"Bernie Owens' book when profound and refreshing experience into the Love and Peace of God. I will recommend this book to all my clients and to the people that attend my many workshops. This book has been written by a man deeply immersed in God and it is an overflow of his profound experience of God. Make sure you read this book."

Fred Cavaiani, psychologist, marriage and
family therapist, spiritual director

"*More Than You Could Ever Imagine: On Our Becoming Divine* is a superb introduction to the Christian spiritual path, from initial conversion to full transformation. Guided by *The Spiritual Exercises of St. Ignatius*, Owens, a Jesuit, presents the basic dynamic of Christian life. Building on Ignatian insights, Owens then borrows classic texts from John of the Cross to present the ultimate goal of the Christian spiritual path—deification or 'becoming divine.' Owens concretely illustrates his insights with examples, many from his own life. Each chapter concludes with reflection questions making it ideal for personal spiritual inspiration as well as for group reflection."

Dick Hauser, SJ
Assistant to the President for Mission
Professor Emeritus of Theology
Creighton University Jesuit Community

"Through this book, Fr. Owens fulfills his goal of providing a rich and comprehensive description of our spiritual journey toward divinization; that is, transformation into God. A seasoned and respected spiritual director and teacher, he draws upon his profound understanding of the spiritual legacies of Ignatius of Loyola, John of the Cross, and Teilhard de Chardin to guide us through the joys and challenges of the spiritual life. Anyone, priest, religious, and member of the laity, looking for a roadmap for their spiritual journey, will find it here."

Patricia Cooney Hathaway
Professor of Spirituality and Systematic Theology
Sacred Heart Major Seminary, Detroit, Michigan
Author of *Weaving Faith and Experience:
A Woman's Perspective*

"*More Than You Could Ever Imagine* is a wise and reliable guidebook to our shared human destiny: the 'great unfolding of our lives, our Passover journey into God' (8). Jesuit Bernie Owens accompanies us step by step through the life-process of gradual 'divinization,' individually and communally, in response to God's surpassing graciousness and love. The author shows a remarkable gift for presenting profound spiritual insights and deep theological truths in accessible and appealing language, using images and experiences from everyday life. Deeply rooted in the Scriptures and the insights of the Spanish mystics Ignatius, Teresa, and John of the Cross, yet thoroughly contemporary, this book should appeal to many readers, and includes reflection questions at the end of each chapter to facilitate group discussion."

Steven Payne, OCD
Principal of Tangaza University College,
Nairobi, Africa

More Than You Could Ever Imagine

On Our Becoming Divine

Bernie Owens, SJ

LITURGICAL PRESS
Collegeville, Minnesota

www.litpress.org

1   2   3   4   5   6   7   8   9

Library of Congress Cataloging-in-Publication Data

Owens, Bernard J.
   More than you could ever imagine / Bernard Owens, SJ.
      pages cm
      ISBN 978-0-8146-4921-3 — ISBN 978-0-8146-4946-6 (ebook)
      1. Deification (Christianity) 2. Mysticism—Catholic Church.   I. Title.

BT767.8.O94   2015
233—dc23

2014024235

To my parents
John Christopher and Bernice Marie Owens

To my friends
Dave Asselin, SJ, and Jules Toner, SJ

To my mentor
Michael J. Buckley, SJ

Contents

ACKNOWLEDGMENTS

I first wish to thank my many friends who often came to the 8 a.m. weekday Mass at Manresa Jesuit Retreat House in Bloomfield Hills, Michigan. Besides them I wish to recognize numerous students who participated in biweekly reading seminars at Manresa, when together we discussed some of the great Christian spiritual classics, especially Ignatian and Carmelite writings. I would hear from both groups, "you should write a book on some of this." Never did I think I would ever have the time to act on their encouraging words.

Then for the 2010–11 academic year Fr. Greg Hyde, superior of the Jesuit community at that time at Manresa, suggested my taking a sabbatical after sixteen years there. Lo and behold, I now had the time to act on these urgings of others to write. Grateful to him for this surprising gift, I moved to another Jesuit community, this one at the University of Detroit Mercy, where I had taught from 1981 to 1994. I was far enough away to get the needed quiet and distance to write but close enough to care for my ailing mother, who would die during the latter part of the sabbatical. I am immensely grateful to the Jesuit superior, Fr. Simon Hendry, and the university's Jesuit community for warmly welcoming me, encouraging me during the inevitable ups and downs of writing, and supporting me during my mother's funeral.

It took me the entire year to write the first draft of the book; much rewriting and editing were still to be done on it when the sabbatical ended. Whatever time I found for this had to be taken during "free time" from the usual responsibilities of leading programs and retreats at Manresa. Sometimes three months would go by before I had any time to return to this project.

A number of friends generously offered to proofread the manuscript and made excellent suggestions: Fred Cavaiani, Michelle Wilbert, Jerry LeCarpentier, Fr. Dan Liderbach, SJ, Lucia Dubois, Rosemary Insley, Robert and Kimberly Jumonville-Moore, Wil Hernandez, Sandy Harding, Fr. Brian Daley, SJ, and the staff at Liturgical Press. I am most grateful for their great support and encouragement, sometimes in the form of blunt advice, but almost always helpful in leading to some sort of improvement.

I thank Mr. Hugh Buchanan, assistant director of Manresa Jesuit Retreat House, and Fr. Bart Murphy, SJ, of Mwangaza Jesuit Spiritual Centre in Nairobi, Kenya, for their invaluable assistance in solving computer challenges. Hugh was also very helpful in my gaining permissions to use certain quotes and the image on the front cover.

Thanks to Mrs. Ann Dillon, longtime friend and work colleague, for sensing my need for encouragement and advice at a time during the earlier stages of this project.

I want to recognize the spirit of community and welcome in the Jesuit communities of both Manresa in Bloomfield Hills and Mwangaza in Nairobi, where I now live and minister.

I must also acknowledge the interns in the Internship in Ignatian Spirituality at Manresa. Their dedication to preparation for ministry and passion for God have greatly inspired me. The interaction I had with more than 350 of them over eighteen years has spurred me on in my desire to write on the topic of this book: our being divinized by God.

I wish to recognize the wonderful colleagues with whom I worked as fellow staff members in the internship: Denise

Anderson, Lucia Dubois, Fr. Benno Kornely, SJ, Margaret Wheeler, Marian Love, Kathy O'Donnell, Artemae Anderson, Paula Dow, Anne Carey, Diane Neville, Gayle McGregor, Sr. Ellen Licavoli, IHM, and Ann Dillon. Their support and friendship sustained me while my desire to write this book grew.

And, of course, the men and women members of the internship's supervision community—too many to name here. I owe so much to their commitment to the interns and the refinement of the internship's supervision process. Their care and professionalism made it possible to hand over more responsibility for the internship when the opportunity came to write this book.

I owe a special word of thanks to some wonderful neighbors, Rick and Kathy Wagoner, who on several occasions loaned me use of their lovely home on Daufuskie Island in South Carolina. It was there that I found inspiration for the title of this book.

Thanks are also due to Fr. Dave Meconi, SJ, Fr. Brian Daley, SJ, Fr. Peter Bernardi, SJ, Sr. Mary Kerber, SSND, Brother Herbert Liebl, SJ, and Mary Carol Conroy for their help in finding certain bibliographical sources and quotes. Joe Koczera, SJ, was very helpful with a detail of this book that unfortunately had to be omitted; Fr. Jim Kubicki, SJ, was helpful with sourcing an image; and Fr. Kevin Culligan, OCD, confirmed my reading and interpretation of some texts of St. John of the Cross cited in this work.

Special thanks to Fr. Peter Bernardi, SJ, Kay Engel, my spiritual director for twenty-four years, Giorgio and Maria Pia Abate, John and Pat Brewster, Joe and Angela Rivello, Carden and Marian Smith, Roger and Vincie Lucido, Mike and Jerilynn Ciletti, Tom Duff, Pamela Prime, Rosalie Hebeler, Isaac Hanna, and Mary McKeon for their longtime gift of friendship and steady encouragement during my writing.

And to my siblings, who have a special place in my heart: John Christopher II, Mary, Pat, and John Thomas. In their unique ways and in what they will know only at the end of this journey to God, they and their families have been a great blessing and support to me.

I am greatly pleased to dedicate this book to five special people in my life. First, to my parents, John Christopher and Bernice Marie Owens. They believed deeply in the mystery of God's love, shared with me their faith in God, and brought me to Christ and his church, its Scriptures, its sacraments, and its remarkable legacy of saints. I will never be able to thank them enough.

Then two Jesuit priests and friends, Dave Asselin, a Canadian who mentored me closely in the text of St. Ignatius of Loyola's *Spiritual Exercises*, and Jules Toner, who opened me up to the treasures of Ignatius's discernment principles. Sometimes Jules and I teamed together for weekend workshops on the discernment of spirits and of God's will. What fond memories I have of both of these Jesuits.

Finally, I dedicate this work to a Jesuit priest and great mentor, Michael J. Buckley. He took me deeply into the poetry and teachings of John of the Cross. I am grateful beyond words for this, as they have become a singular gift in my life. Saint John has had a profound impact on my own personal walk with God, and his poetry, wisdom, passion, and vision of our future in God have greatly informed my ministries of preaching, teaching, spiritual direction, and retreat guidance. It is St. John's vision especially that has inspired me to write this book, so that what I consider this best part of the Good News is made available and (I hope) understandable to those who have not yet read his writings or found them to be somewhat daunting.

INTRODUCTION

"Abba . . . Ah-bah! . . . AAAhh-baahh!!" A child's insistent voice sounded just outside my nighttime door. I was trying to fall asleep on a hot August night in Tiberias, Israel, near the shores of the Lake of Galilee, when I was brought to full attention by this voice. Soon steps sounded down the stairs, then some muted voices, and finally quiet. But I could not get back to sleep for quite some time. I was in tears, haunted by that child's calling. It had struck a deep chord in my spirit. I knew this is the respectful and sometimes affectionate way in which Jews and many Arabs, whether they are children or adults, address their fathers. I knew from my studies of the Christian Scriptures how powerful that name was for Jesus.

A number of thoughts ran through my mind: how Jesus spoke that name so openly and upset many with what seemed to them to be a much too familiar—almost blasphemous—way of addressing God, and then great wonder about this child calling out for his or her father in that moment. I wanted to meet the child, if at all possible. As unlikely as that possibility seemed, I was hoping to meet the child because I was quite curious about meeting present-day Jews who speak the same words that Jesus spoke, at least this word that meant so much to him. But deeper than that, I wanted to meet up with this little one because in some vague sense I had a hunch that this child—in its crying out—was like my own self and that to meet the child would be, just maybe, an opportunity to discover something important in myself.

The next morning, after breakfast, while on my way back to my room I had the happy fortune of meeting the father and child along with two older brothers. The child was a girl about three years old. She and her family had come from the city of Haifa to vacation that week at the lake. The father spoke very good English and wore the traditional Jewish yamaka or skullcap on the top of his head.[1] The two brothers, one about twelve years old and the other seven or eight, looked curiously at me, a tall American, but remained silent, obviously hesitant about their ability to speak English.

The little girl's manner amazed me. She chose to hide behind her father's legs and peek out at me from time to time while holding on to the smallest finger of one of her daddy's hands. For me the gestures of her holding her father's little finger while numerous times peeking out at me and pulling back were unforgettable. I remarked to myself, "O, my God, there I am; there we all are!" This little child had shown me something so true about my own self, and, I believe, about each one of us.

I was touched to see the security and trust she felt with her father. For her he was safe; he was someone she knew and could trust. He was her Abba. And I? I was entirely an unknown, very "other," almost a head taller than her father, and speaking a language she did not recognize. In one moment she was curious and would peek out from behind. In the next moment it was too much for her and she would pull back, letting her father completely block my view. If my eyes caught hers, she would immediately pull back, even if I smiled. This happened some six to eight times during our conversation. She was so beautiful, so human, so real. I wondered whether this is how all of us experience each other too much of the time. But I was more taken with how her manner seemed to be the usual way in which we relate to God.

After I said my good-bye and made sure I said good-bye to this shy little one, my thoughts went back a number of times to this touching encounter. The memory of that first night of my pilgrimage to the Holy Land still rings with this little girl's cry to her Abba, a respectful, even affectionate call for her father's help. As a visitor to the Lake of Galilee in 1996, I had been moved to recall how powerful, for Jesus, was that one word, Abba. Throughout the rest of the pilgrimage and for weeks thereafter I would ponder what I had experienced, thanks to this child.

My reflections gathered around how all of us, whether child or adult, seek the assurance and security of a reliable love. We want to be able to hold on, to be anchored by what is imaged in the littlest finger of the father. We need to be touched, so to speak, to be welcomed and cared for. Most fundamentally, we long to be known and loved for who we are and then eventually to give ourselves to some love that genuinely values us. We may adopt a way of life that for the most part hides this foundational reality from ourselves. Yet it is branded in our souls and will make itself known in various ways. Powerfully this "fingerprint" of the Creator in our depths will remind us of where we have come from and what life is about.

The demeanor of this little girl said to me that these needs had been met in her, at least for the moment and to the degree that she was capable of receiving. But like us all, she would eventually have to leave her place of security, peek out, and not pull back at what was coming next in her life if she were to live at all. Like us all, she would have to choose over and over to trust the love of her divine Abba and move out to meet the world and risk loving in the face of the challenges of each day.

The lives of each of us are one great unfolding, similar to a rose plant that begins as a humble and fragile bare root. The plant has to receive adequate sun and go through stages of first manifesting tender shoots, then stronger, thicker branches, leaves, and eventually its buds. It will have to be fertilized, watered regularly, freed from weeds and insects, and also pruned. Over time, it will develop into a large bush with abundant blossoms, displaying beauty and giving delight to those who gaze at them. It is this final state of our development that

I especially want to address in this book. What we are to become, in Christ, is far more than we could ever ask for or imagine. A glimpse of this has moved innumerable hearts to an abiding sense of awe and praise of God. A description of this glorious destiny and fullness to come, however, requires our looking at the most important spiritual experiences that lead up to such a climax; these experiences are critical to our unfolding. By considering them in the context of the entire spiritual journey, we will more fully appreciate the final outcome of this wondrous process.

Perhaps the most fitting metaphor for my describing this transformation process we undergo is the Passover. The Passover is the controlling motif used in the Bible to tell the story of the Hebrew-Israelites' liberation from slavery and their coming into a new promised land. It images their own unfolding as they come alive to who they are as a people; it contains so many stories of individual Israelites growing into their inheritance as sons and daughters of God and finding the meaning and joy of their lives in serving God.

The story of our Passover or unfolding starts long before we are conceived. It begins with God forming a covenant with Abraham and the Hebrew people,[2] later with Moses and King David,[3] and intensifies during the times of the Jewish prophets, the psalmist writer, and wisdom authors.[4] Finally, it reaches its climax in Jesus, especially during the last hours of his life. As though to reveal the longings of God to give himself to us, the Gospel of St. Luke quotes Jesus at the Last Supper: "It is with desire that I have desired to eat this Passover with you before I suffer" (22:15).[5]

To say "with desire have I desired" is a very Jewish way of expressing what lies deep within. Jesus is revealing the depths of God as well as of his own Heart when he says this. He speaks these words while knowing he is soon to die; they come from a part of himself that matters most to him, what is most true and beautiful in himself. They are spoken to anyone of us willing to listen; he is inviting us to make a journey with him, a Passover into God, and become all we can be.

What might this Passover look like? Very briefly, if we say yes to this invitation, it will involve God and ourselves first getting to know each other, and then becoming good friends and sharing together our joys and struggles. In time, if we keep saying yes, the relationship will open out into a deeper love for each other. Finally, if we continue to grow in love, we will be moved to invest everything in a communion characterized by total mutuality. It will be a complete giving of each to the other, for time and eternity. We will have "passed over" into the life and Heart of God and know a fullness and joy beyond all our expectations or hopes.

The marvelous story of our Passover is a process of our passing over from fear and shame, from self-centered thinking and from choices that lead to loneliness and death—to a freedom to live with hope and peace for something much more fulfilling and enlivening than what our egos propose. Egos tend toward pride and envy, greed and lust, hatred and self-centeredness. God's invitation, however, is an offer to live differently; it is an opportunity to discover the life-giving world of relationships with God, neighbor, and our true self. From the depths of God, who is Gracious Mystery,[6] Jesus speaks to anyone willing to accept and trust this unparalleled gift that every human being is seeking, so often in all the wrong places. It is a gift much richer than we could ever anticipate. Maybe this is why so many people, even some Christians, find it too good to be true, too extreme to be credible what God promises us as the meaning and fulfillment of our life. In the face of much skepticism and cynicism, the gospels, the letters of St. Paul, and especially the Christian mystics proclaim this gift as nothing less than the Heart of God—pierced, opened, and given completely to anyone willing to receive. They proclaim a new life for us, a transformed self, a new being that becomes divine.

Love that goes to these lengths to love us, to be this vulnerable, to suffer so much, to be pierced and completely given, can frighten us. We can be afraid of where this kind of love would take us and what it would cost and ask from us in return. Yet it is a gentle love, always respectful, never forcing, and so patient in waiting for our response right up to the end of our life. Coming from God's depths, such love longs to give itself completely. To accept this humble but frequently issued invitation is to begin a journey meant to lead someday to God and ourselves sharing fully in an eternal Passover meal and relating as equals.

In Jesus God promises in our lives a transformation so great that at the end of the process we will know as God knows and love as God loves. We will perceive and relish all of creation as God sees and enjoys it. We will "feel" as God "feels," rejoicing in whatever God rejoices in. We will be so transformed in Christ that we will give ourselves to God as totally as God gives himself to us. In essence, this is what it means to say we will become divine, living the life of God as God lives it.

Is this too much to believe, too good to be true? And just what does it all mean and how could such ever happen? Surely, this vision and promise of God is beyond anything we might imagine. Yet the Christian Scriptures and mystics declare without any hesitation that this is our destiny, our ultimate treasure, the "pearl of great price" waiting for us to discover and claim for our own (Matt 13:46). The Christian mystics, like some in other religions, are always talking about God's life in us. They are in one way or another stunned and held with great awe, sometimes trembling at what they see to be our destiny. They have glimpsed the ineffable with the eye of their heart, just as the apostles Peter, James, and John did on Mount Tabor when they witnessed the transfiguration of Jesus (Matt 17:1-8; Mark 9:2-8; Luke 9:28-36). Overwhelmed with awe and forced to their knees by the brilliant manifestation of his divine nature, they nevertheless knew in some sense that the same transformation and transfiguration process was to happen to them someday in God's providence. They knew that they too would radiate with this same powerful love from the center of their being.[7] They had glimpsed something of the amazing future that awaits anyone who will trust and go with this process of passing over into God.

In Jesus the One who is Gracious Mystery becomes one of us and experiences what it is like to be human in all our glory and pain. In laying down his life he gives us his own Heart and invites us, when we are ready, to give him our own hearts. What an exchange this is, his Heart for our own! In doing so he creates within us the capacity to live fully the life of God and, at the same time, to be the fullness of who we are, of all we are being created to be.

This process involves our being purified in heart and enlightened with new knowledge, understanding, and wisdom. We get stretched far beyond our initial abilities and awarenesses. We are weaned from our fears, from having to be too cautious and choosing to hide or cover up at times. We are coaxed beyond our habits of peeking out at life with our frightened child's eyes from behind our titles and possessions. We are freed more and more to trust life, to trust ourselves as good and as loved. While before we were clinging to the little finger of what we had let become our god, over time we come to know the One whom now we stay close to, not with anxiety but with trust, with love, gratitude, and inner peace. Our spirit and the actions of our soul undergo, then, a remarkable deepening and likening to God. By the end of this process we realize our God-given potential and beauty in being divinized, the fullness of what God promises us.

It is with desire that God has desired each of us to know what he knows and to love as he loves, to taste and savor life as he does, with the joy that is his. This gesture can be imaged in terms of a heavenly meal that God is readying us to share in. He prepares us throughout our lives and even beyond until we are fully transformed. When that great and final day comes, Christ Jesus will hand over to God all of us, his brothers and sisters and the rest of creation, so that "God may be all in all" (1 Cor 15:28). God will have finally gathered us, his family, into one . . . into the Christ, at the banquet table of eternal life. What a day that will be!

Thanks to our having been converted in heart and mind and experiencing a radical change of values and priorities (Phil 3:7-14); thanks to our having been freed from living from many desires that conflict, divide, and scatter our souls; thanks now to our being freed to live from our center and always seek "the one thing necessary" (see Luke 10:38-42), we will find emerging in our hearts a single-focused longing. It will echo the longings of Jesus expressed at the first Eucharist. We, individually and as a human race, will say in return, "It is with desire that we have desired to eat this Passover with you. We too long for this deepest of communions and a complete giving of ourselves to you."

Thanks to this wondrous transformation we undergo during our Passover journey, we will be empowered to love as we were loved at that first Eucharist. Thanks to the gift of God declared in 2 Peter 1:4 (we will "share in the divine nature") and celebrated in this too often forgotten saying of the Fathers of the church—*the Divine became human so that the human may become Divine*—our God-given potentials and deepest hopes will be realized. In an astonishing way we will become what Eucharist is, poured out completely for God and for all creation, forever and ever. We will become what we receive, the Body and Blood of Christ.

❖   ❖   ❖

This book maps out the main experiences and describes many of the rich blessings we are given during this great unfolding of our lives, our Passover journey into God. Themes of the Bible highlight God's works in these experiences, especially those presented in the Spiritual Exercises of St. Ignatius of Loyola.[8] The last two chapters attempt to give some description of what we will become, what we will "look like," so to speak, at the end of our journey, both individually and as a human race. For this I rely especially upon the teachings of St. Paul, the writings of St. John of the Cross, the sixteenth-century Carmelite poet and mystic, and those of the twentieth-century Jesuit priest-scientist Pierre Teilhard de Chardin. I must also credit my dear friend and mentor Jules Toner, a fellow Jesuit and great teacher of discernment. His insights on friendship and communion have proven to be very helpful when reflecting on life for those in the communion of saints.

What I am addressing is what I consider among the most important and beautiful themes of Christian theology and spirituality, namely, our being divinized. This has been a central theme of the liturgies and theologies of the Eastern church from the earliest centuries of Christianity, but hardly as much in the Western church. It seems that in the West the cultural changes wrought through the Renaissance and especially of the eighteenth-century Enlightenment movement led to a heavy, unbalanced emphasis on what is rational and empirical, along with a loss of interest in the more mystical dimensions of the spiritual life. Only in more recent times has the theme of divinization regained significant interest in the West. It is a topic that has always captivated my wonder and has often stirred me deeply during prayer, also when I am teaching and conversing with friends. My study of the spirituality of divinization has confirmed my intuition of how this same process unfolds even in the lives of many who are not baptized Christians. It dismays me that so few Christians ever hear about this central and exciting teaching; or if they do, the topic is scarcely developed for them with any depth.

My hope is that this book will present with significant depth the theme of divinization and major pieces of the process leading to it. May it deepen your sense of wonder at how sacred and beautiful is the journey we are all making, baptized Christians and others as well. With this purpose in mind I have tried to use language friendly to the layperson and to those who are not scholars and academicians. I envision the book being an excellent source of spiritual reading for many kinds of Christian individuals. It could be most engaging for book-club and faith-sharing groups, and a good sequel for those who have finished the RCIA process, RENEW groups, and participants in the Alpha Course. Reflection questions have been added to the end of each chapter to make this use more possible. Hopefully, many pastors of churches as well as leaders of faith formation and ministry preparation programs will find the text a useful resource for their preaching and teaching. Psychotherapists might also recommend it to clients who are open to spirituality. Finally, I am hoping that the general seeker of spiritual truth and hope, whether Christian or not, will find this book helpful in his or her own search for the One from whom each and all of us come.

Chapter One

THE JOURNEY BEGINS IN EARNEST

We can live many years yet not really live. We can pass through the greater part or even all of our life unaware of who we are and why we are. We can be a great success according to the norms of the public media or the company for which we work. We can possess health and wealth, long life, an education, the pleasures and joys of marriage and family or many friends but still not have a sense of the meaning of our life.

What is it, then, that "kick-starts" our life's journey and provides its centerpiece and integrating factor? What has to happen that will free us to come really alive and be filled with purpose? The best literature I read, including the Bible as well as life testimonies and the story of my own life, tells me that the pivotal event in any person's life is our waking up to and accepting a great love in our life. Yet it is more than just waking up to this great love that has to happen. It is absolutely essential that we also welcome this love. We need to receive it and be moved by it, recognizing its rightness for us and letting it make its claim on us. We have to let it lead us beyond our own small sense of self and prompt us to respond, honor, serve, be shaped by it, and enjoy the mutuality it offers. This is the moment our life's journey or Passover begins in earnest. Before this, our life by comparison might be likened to having "our engine much of the time in neutral"; or maybe our life was largely a sleepwalk, or worse, a life that was spiritually anemic, even sick unto death.

The gift of this great love is offered to us from our earliest days in a myriad of ways: in parents and family, in nature, in the arts, in people we meet along the way, and in our own self-discovery of the talents as well as limitations our bodies, minds, and hearts place in front of us. Each encounter of our life speaks God's love to us: I give this to you because I love you and want to share myself with you. You are mine and you are "precious in my eyes" (see Isa 43:1, 4; Gal 2:20). Every human experience, in fact, is potentially an experience of love's presence, the depth dimension that is the basis or foundation of all that is.

Yet we can go on and on, taking in all of these gifts but failing to recognize their Source, or at most, paying mere lip service to this Source. We might be moved by a significant love in our life, a spouse or child or great friend, and yet not make the connection with their Source. It is true that our journey will have begun insofar as we have responded with love and gratitude to a significant love in our life. Such experiences, however, await a deeper discovery on our part, an awakening to this faithful presence as Someone inviting mutuality. Once we recognize the veiled presence of this holy One and develop a habit of responding, our life opens out into a new fullness and depth that was not there before. It becomes, now more than ever, a Passover journey into God.

By acknowledging and welcoming this Someone we begin to make room in our depths for a life-changing relationship. We no longer live as a completely autonomous individual in charge of our life. Rather, we have awakened to the great truth that we have been loved by Someone who knows us personally, by name, and cares for us. We begin to live the reality that each of us is part of a "we," part of a unique relationship with the divine Source of everything. Because of our new consciousness, we learn to trust that we are never alone, even if we feel alone. Gracious Mystery is deeper than any and all of our feelings because he has come to live with us in our center and make our center his home (John 14:23). In time we learn that this Gracious One is even grateful to us for our "yes" and treasures this new friendship.

God as Teacher

Like a wonderfully skilled teacher, this mysterious One takes us step by step on a journey with a specific direction. We awaken to a sense of being led in a spirit of love; we see more than ever what innumerable gifts this divine Gift-giver has been showering on us. Such a great outpouring prepares for our saying yes to living with this divine Friend in mutual love and friendship. The eye of our heart is opening and is increasingly appreciating the love and affirmation behind the many gestures of care, protection, healing, guidance, and inspiration received over the years. Gratitude and awe emerge. Reverence and respect pour out spontaneously. Wonder for this One who has been in our life from its beginnings grows within us as we realize we have done nothing to earn such joy.

The gifts of creation and our own creation are seen in a new light. We begin to appreciate this Gracious Mystery creating all things, whether cosmic or microscopic in its dimensions. We find ourselves marveling at the infinite spaces and beauty the astrophysicists show us. At the same time they speak about how tiny our earth is in relation to the rest of the cosmos. We stagger with wonder as geologists and astronomers tell us our earth was born over four billion years ago and that our galaxy is one of billions in an ever-expanding universe. We are moved to praise and wonder at the delicacy and ordered beauty of the world under the microscope.

We are overwhelmed with the majesty of divine Love as well as the minute and particular nature of that love, which has included us in it. Our sense of reverence and adoration deepens, especially when we begin to look at the circumstances of our own conception, birth, and our years of growing up. More and more we grow in wonder, gratitude, and praise for how all of this is a great gift to us, as if we were the sole object of the love of this mysterious Gift-giver. And so we are drawn, attracted to know and love this Creator who first knew and loved us. Our journey, our Passover into God, is now marked by new desires and hopes that urge us to explore this relationship with God.

This wondrous process deepens. God comes closer than being just our creator. In Jesus this Gracious One becomes one of us creatures, becomes more invested, gets into our skin, so to speak, and experiences our life from within. How humble is such love, to get down on our level and relate to us in our human ordinariness. It reminds one of Søren Kierkegaard's parable of the prince who woos a peasant girl by donning the clothes of a peasant.[1] Who, then, is this God who wants to feel what we feel, know as we know, and love as we love? Just as the best speakers know their audience—their history, culture, preoccupations, and present situation—God knows us in giving us Jesus. God adapts to our situation with its countless particularities. In Jesus God speaks love and hope to us as never before. Jesus is that divine Word coming from the deepest part of Gracious Mystery and is proclaimed in the midst of the ordinary as well as in the struggles of our daily existence.

This is not what the peoples of the world expect, however. The history of religions shows a much greater readiness to believe in a God who is transcendent, far above us, rather than one who shares in the joys and frustrations of mortal humanity. A God who would sit with us, laugh and weep with us, eat, struggle, suffer, and die like us is simply too much for most in this world. It is all too inappropriate because God is commonly thought of as all powerful and immune from death and the foibles of humanity. ~~Yet the stunning, shocking truth is that this all-powerful God is, at the same time, a humble and vulnerable God.~~ In Jesus God fully embraces humanity, all its glory as well as its ignominy and messiness. We run from our messiness and shame, from what we fear and what we are powerless to control. There are some things in life we do not want to face. ~~But in Jesus, God become human, we are loved for who we are, even with all the sad and awful situations we bring on ourselves.~~ God chooses to enter into what we most fear and loathe about ourselves.

It is quite awe inspiring to realize that Gracious Mystery moves from being our creator to becoming a creature like ourselves in the person of Jesus. But it leaves us virtually speechless to witness this One who in Jesus chooses to embrace that part of our creaturely nature we most fear and want to flee: suffering and death. In Jesus God chooses to be with us in all of our struggles, in our experiences of powerlessness and failure, in our humiliations and losses, and ultimately in the loss of everything in death. This is the mystery of his cross! Is there any god like this God? Can we even begin to fathom how deep, how great is this love embracing us? We can be, at the same time, both fascinated by it and left trembling with a fear of it.

God Hidden in Humility

A God so humble raises the question, How can one submitting to indignity and humiliation be God? It is foolishness. Yet those who have suffered significant injustice or personal harm often recognize this gesture of Gracious Mystery in Jesus as the supreme act of compassionate love. To be shown a love this vulnerable, courageous, and faithful to the end has moved millions over the years to faith in this One as the only God. Eventually, the whole world will stop shielding its eyes and will finally face this ultimate expression of love . . . and fall to its knees and adore (Phil 2:5-11).

Once we see this unprecedented expression of love, once we hear this Word spoken in our depths and recognize how loved we are, we will want, more than ever, to love back. We will want to give ourselves with great generosity to this gracious, gracious Mystery of love, of life, and of hope for the world. We will experience our journey into God taking on a greater energy and desire. The broad outlines of a new self being given to us by God are taking shape!

Scriptural Examples

Let me be more specific about this.

There comes a day in God's kindly providence when we hear in our depths God's Word of love spoken personally: "With age-old love I have loved you" (Jer 31:3), so much do you mean to me. I nurtured and taught you, guarded you as the apple of my eye. As the eagle spreads its wings to carry its young, I bore you on my shoulders (see Deut 32:10-11), so much do I love you. "You are precious in my eyes . . . and I love you" (Isa 43:4). Truly I have formed your inmost being and knit you in your mother's womb. Your soul also I have known full well, nor was your frame unknown to me when I made you in secret (see Ps 139:13-15). It is as if God were speaking, "Do you not understand what I am saying to you? I give you what is my best and most loved, my only-begotten Son, your elder brother who saves you from being unloved, from self-doubt, from hopelessness and self-rejection. He is Heart of my Heart, and I give him to you *so that you may know what you mean to me*. In his living, dying, and rising you will see that my Heart can never forget you, no matter what you do! I can *never* forget you because I am God, I am love. I cannot be any other way. Do you believe me? Will you accept me? Will you let me in . . . into your heart and mind and life?"

When we hear such words of God and let them sound in our center, we realize that each of us is much like the little three-year-old girl. We are invited by love to come out from behind the ways we have hidden ourselves, our hearts and longings for truth and trustworthy relationship. We begin to realize that there is this surprising, undeserved love that has given us his life so that we might live. We awaken to how loved we are, known and accepted for who we are despite all our shortcomings and problems. We happily discover a love unlike any other love: unconditional, personal, and lasting for all times.

Such a personal love is the foundation of a new existence, the beginnings of what the biblical prophet Isaiah and St. Paul call a new creation. In this new order Jesus the Christ is the firstborn, and we begin, perhaps, to sense something of the place we are being given in it. Without this foundation there is no spiritual identity, no sense of who we are. In such a sorry state we end up drifting through life.

To know we are loved in this all-embracing way changes everything. It energizes us to say an enthusiastic yes to this divine invitation to the Passover journey. The great unfolding begins to happen. We open up as if to a great light, warm and reassuring. We start out on this journey knowing now that we are not alone but are accompanied by this light. We feel known and wanted, accepted and welcomed.

Jesus tries to teach us this when he taught his disciples the prayer called the Our Father.[2] This prayer is supremely the prayer of Jesus. He urges us to make his prayer our own prayer by praying it over and over again and growing into its attitudes and values. If we do so, we will in time relate to God and neighbor differently because we will have come to relate to our own selves differently. The Spirit of Jesus will unlock inside us new spiritual strengths and enable us to overcome any testing, survive any crisis, or encounter any humiliation. It is a prayer that comes from the center, the deepest part of Jesus where he is in communion with God. He knows God as Abba or Daddy and knows himself as the beloved of Abba. This is the source of his joy and the very reason he lives as he lives. Jesus gives us this prayer, then, with the invitation to name and own his Abba as our Abba, our Father.

I am well aware that because of Christ and the triune God he reveals, God is beyond all names and can be addressed in many other reverent, loving ways: Imma, Em or Amma, our Mother, for example. The point is that in Christ's Spirit we can pray to God with names of either gender. All names are analogously applied. In this prayer Jesus encourages you and me to open up to a relationship with the One who is Gracious Mystery, who is as tender as a most caring parent with his or her favorite child. Jesus is virtually daring us to let ourselves be held close by God, heart to Heart, and to experience this God as our God. It would bear some semblance to the little girl holding on to the little finger of her Abba but now with courage and strength to go forward in life. The choice is ours to make.

What a struggle it is, however, for many of us to get past our fear of such intimacy and be free enough to trust it. Maybe it is a fear that this intimacy is not real; or maybe it is a fear of our later being betrayed or used and pushed away. For some the obstacle is our sense that "I don't belong here, I don't deserve this" because parts of our past are not yet forgiven and healed.[3] However, once we begin to trust this love and claim it for ourselves as a gift freely and genuinely given, we start discovering the beauty, goodness, and truth that lie inside ourselves. We see something of what God sees when looking at us and begin to trust in the great value God has placed on our lives. This moves us to faith in God and hope in the tomorrows to come. Like an infant who has gotten past struggling to stand on its wobbly feet, we now are able to walk, at least in a beginner's sense, with confidence in our life. For the first time we know something of who we are.

So the Our Father prayer has become our prayer. To pray it with such consciousness is to be taken to the core of our true selves, our best selves. At this sacred point in our depths each of us knows and trusts to some degree that we are loved and cherished as a son or daughter of the divine Abba given uncon-ditionally. Sad to say, this is for many people too good to believe in or trust. Yet it is our center and the only place where we will discover who we are. The One who lives and makes his home in this center woos us through the Spirit, coaxes us, and patiently waits for us to discover there this treasure of our true selves living in communion and never alone.

Those who cannot see themselves as God's treasure can some-times recognize it in another human being who has embraced such a love in his or her life. Perhaps it is in and through another person, whether in friendship, in a love that is married or celibate, or maybe in reading an account of his or her life,[4] that we can finally have the courage to risk, to let go and believe in the com-munion of this same Gracious Mystery and our own true selves.

A Personal Example

For myself, there have been numerous blessings in my life but none as strong and formative as one that came in my thirty-third year, four months before I was ordained a Catholic priest. This graced moment was given to me during an eight-day silent retreat I was making. In the afternoon of the fifth day I intended to pray on a gospel scene in the public life of Jesus. But random reflections from past months and years about the circumstances of my parents' dating, marrying, and then giving birth to me as their firstborn came rushing into my consciousness. I had pondered such facts before, but this time they seized my consciousness with an unprecedented power and completely overwhelmed me.

My father was the oldest male in his family. He had six other siblings. Unfortunately, his father died rather suddenly when he was only eleven years old. This tragedy left him as the "man of the family." He now had to take on adult responsibilities well before his time and help manage an eighty-acre farm. Dyslexic and struggling with school, he quit after the eighth grade and went to work as an apprentice to an electrician. His earnings helped his younger siblings buy their clothes and get through school. Not until he was in his early thirties did he seriously begin to date. Typical of the firstborn male in an Irish family, he waited until he saw his younger siblings grown and launched in their own lives. He also cared for his mother until she died before he began searching for a life partner. He could have taken a different path. He could have insisted that others in the family assume many or all of his responsibilities while he started his own life. He could have put himself first but did not.

On that day, I was so struck by my father's choices before he married. I sensed so strongly that if he had chosen to "start his life" much earlier than he did, I most probably would never have existed. His "yes" to his life as it was given to him, his sacrifice, so to speak, became priceless in my own life story.

A very similar sense of profound gratitude came to me as I considered my mother's early years. She was the oldest female in a family of nine children. In 1934, in the middle of the Great Depression, she graduated from high school. She wanted to enter religious life as a Sister of St. Joseph. But her mother quite strongly asserted the needs of the large family, insisting that a greater financial burden would weigh on the family if she entered the convent. She was needed, she was told, to go to work and bring home a paycheck rather than draw upon the limited income of her father.

Like my father, my mother could have insisted on a different path than the one required of her by the economic constraints of her family. At least, to my mind, she was not entirely determined to take the path her parents chose for her. What I came to realize was that either of my parents could have chosen to live beyond the needs of their families, but neither of them did so. What a powerful, emotionally charged awareness this led me to in that moment. I felt swept up by a love that branded in my soul how valued and desired I am by God. I sensed I am not an "anybody" in a world of over seven billion human beings, but a very particular someone known by name, welcomed, and rejoiced in.

Never before had I been affirmed like this. I sobbed for what seemed like forty minutes! My thoughts fixed on the possibility that if either of my parents had rejected the situation and had chosen to go his or her own way, I almost certainly would never have existed. I became more aware than ever before that the gift of one's existence is distinct from and prior to the gift of one's birth. So even if I had been miscarried or aborted, I would still exist forever. There poured out of me, then, an overwhelming sense of being wanted and loved—deeply, deeply loved. As I said to my retreat guide with whom I shared this blessing, "I know beyond the shadow of a doubt that I am not a mistake; I am not just an 'anybody' in a seemingly impersonal, sometimes cold world. Rather, I am very much wanted, welcomed, and chosen by God. God knows me by name. I know who I am and to whom I belong. I know where my home is." And then I wept, with deepest joy.

Later, after catching my breath, I thought, "I want this blessing for everyone in this world. I want everyone to know that they are this loved, that they are known by name and have a place, a home in God's Heart . . . I am absolutely sure God wants this as well." I felt that day and many times thereafter a renewed sense of dedicating my life to making this possible for as many people as I could reach in my life. Jesus wants people to know his Abba Father as their Abba Father as well, that each of us is a son or daughter of his, precious in his eyes and glorious (see Isa 43:4, 6). This is what I want to do as well, however, wherever, whenever I can.

The Footprints of God in Our Own Life

The love of God is relentless. God is always speaking to us, always affirming us in the midst of our day, through creation and in our life stories, no matter how troubled our life might have been so far. Sooner or later there hopefully come self-reflective moments when, with the grace of God, we make connections and notice specific experiences in our lives of God's presence and love for us—such as in people being good and kind to us or in our efforts bearing fruit in the lives of others. We might see the hand of God in the rewards that come our way in having trusted or having been willing to risk for the sake of others. We might notice this divine Presence, this Gracious Mystery, sparing us in times of grave danger or welling up inside us with joy and deep peace. Sometimes it can come in something as simple as a beautiful sunset or in the rise of a full moon, in a walk with our dog in the woods, or in our admiring the flowers and vegetables in the garden we have been cultivating. Other divine visitations may come in an experience of family at the dinner table, in an enjoyable conversation with a loved one, or in experiencing success in our efforts to reconcile with someone we have hurt or been hurt by. It can accompany our feeling satisfaction at finishing well a job or responsibility, in experiencing a loss or failure, in the playing of some music, in seeing a movie, in having a great workout at the gym, or in sharing in a game of cards. We can also be touched by this gracious Presence when coming to accept ourselves as we are, at least more than we did before.

This love has always been there and always will be present in every moment. For those who know how to see, who live with some spirit of gratitude and childlike wonder, everything hints at the presence of this gracious, loving Mystery. Whether we come to such an awareness in a moment of quiet or in a thunderclap experience does not matter. What does matter is that we have awakened to Divine Love who loves us deeply, personally, and in an amazing variety of ways. This Presence is a certain depth dimension speaking and acting in all the arenas of our life: self, other individuals, and social realities; animals, plants, and mineral creation. The gift of noticing this depth dimension in these arenas, in the relationships formed there, and then responding in faith: this is what launches us in earnest on our great life journey of passing over into God. And that is all that matters in the beginning.

Questions for Discussion and Faith-Sharing

1. Can you name a time or event in your life when you woke up to a great love that started you on your own Passover journey? What was that like? What has been your response?

2. Take time to reflect on your family tree before you were born. Name instances of God's love preparing for your coming.

3. Name what differences there might be in a relationship where you know God as "God" versus knowing God as "Abba," or by your special name for God.

4. What might "receiving a new self" imply for your life?

5. Find on the internet or elsewhere a picture of Michelangelo's fresco of God creating Adam. Look closely at the tension in the index fingers and hands of both of them. What does this stir in you, particularly about your own creation?

Chapter Two

LIBERATED FROM SLAVERY

Yes, God is love manifest in our personal histories, in the people around us, in the animals and plants we cherish, in nature, and even in our setbacks, sufferings, and losses. In all of this it is God's great joy to love us. However, this does not mean that all of our experiences with God will be sweet and pleasant. Being loved first opens us to the One loving us, as the sunflower responds to the morning sun. In time love will also expose in us, like an intense spotlight can, whatever is not loving. It will unmask what is not truthful or good or loving in our hearts and thinking. This love will challenge and eventually make impossible the avoidance of anything we are hiding from or choosing to disrespect or hate. It will mirror back issues and moments in our own history not in harmony with love, with the goodness and integrity of our neighbor, and with the truth of our own being. Before, we may have explained what we have done or avoided doing as simply "sowing wild oats" or "just growing up." We may not have acknowledged some things we have done for what they are—namely, sin—until we awakened to God.

There is a Someone, a loving, caring Presence who has been singularly good and kind to us, caring and faithful over the years. This powerful, inescapable truth puts us in touch with an embarrassing truth about ourselves: namely, we have failed to love this Someone in return, as is evident in our lack of caring, or self-centeredness, or ingratitude. Sin, then, is about relationship that has not been honored or respected when it deserves to be. It is about not loving back the One who first loved us, and loved us like no other. This condition is part of our truth, unpleasant to consider, but necessary to own if we are to become free.

Most people think of sin as an act, as something we do or fail to do. Yet, if we are reflective about human motivation, we will recognize that underlying these selfish choices is a radical weakness and a powerlessness that so often sabotages us. We discover that even before sin is something we do or fail to do, it is something mysterious that underlies the way we are. This condition seems to characterize the state of human existence—not that we were created this way, but something seriously damaging happened to humanity from the earliest of times; something skewed us and the overall direction of the God-given energies of our person. Whatever the cause, it has left us prone to fear, mistrust, and an overall self-centered approach to the way we live our lives. We want control, we want our own security, and, painfully enough, we want the esteem of others before the good of our neighbor or of God.[1] We make our own fail-safe, protective system and, like the little girl hiding behind her father's legs, choose to live this way while trying by ourselves to closely manage our life or just let a lot of it pass us by.

Looking Deeper at Sin

Paul Tillich, the Lutheran theologian of the mid-twentieth century, corroborates this insight when he offers a profound description of our human condition before God enters our situation through Jesus. He describes sin, before it is an act, as a condition of our being.[2] It is characterized as a split within our selves, something of a separation or fundamental alienation of our selves from our true selves. We are neither happy nor accepting of who we are. We know just enough not to like or accept ourselves. We want to be someone else. Even more, we want to escape being limited and dependent. This distressed spirit expresses itself sometimes in envying others. At other times we are jealous or greedy, angry or arrogant, impatient or pretending to be other than who we really are.[3] This "dis-ease" with ourselves leads to a separation or alienation from our neighbor, whether individuals or groups, as well as with the animal, plant, and mineral arenas of life. We cannot relate well or at all to these others because we cannot relate well to our own true selves. This lack of self-acceptance prompts as well an unhealthy relationship with God. We either ignore God or try to manipulate God in various ways as we "create" God in our own distorted image and likeness. There is, then, a threefold alienation that describes this sinful condition: separation of self from self, separation of self from neighbor, and separation of self from God. This constitutes our fallen state or the human condition before the coming of God's love and acceptance in Jesus.

This inner drama seems to be characteristic of the lives of so many people. In one degree or other it characterizes every one of us.[4] This inner brokenness and lack of peace is actually the root of all unhealed relationships, a condition that begs for help. It is a situation we do not appreciate until we have attempted on our own some of the many ways humans throughout history have tried to extricate and heal themselves. However, we soon experience the futility of such efforts and our radical powerlessness to save ourselves. It is something only God in Jesus can do for us.

The Judeo-Christian Scriptures point to what we humans need if we are to be freed from this condition. First, the Ten Commandments are given as guidelines to warn us to avoid the basic acts of disobedience against God, neighbor, and self. Specifically, they counsel against idolatry, cursing and blasphemy, disrespect and ingratitude, violence, lust, stealing, and lying. They forbid gossip and the harming of people's reputations; they admonish against envy and greed as well as excess in drinking and eating.

Then we are given the wisdom and guidance found in the eight Beatitudes (Matt 5:3-12), the centerpiece or core of Jesus's teachings. These sayings exhort us to a way of being that fosters God's life in our own selves. They image Jesus himself and give us a sketch of the transformed self that God means to give us.

The commandments focus on behaviors, but, more importantly, the Beatitudes emphasize the attitudes and values underlying behaviors. In the Beatitudes Jesus encourages dispositions of faith, hope, and charity. They warn against arrogance and trusting in ourselves instead of in God, against being impatient and coercive. They urge us to be peacemakers, merciful, gentle in manner, caring for those who suffer and being eager for what is just, letting God take the lead and being single-hearted. God is frank yet respectful in telling us the humbling truth about ourselves, as any reputable doctor would inform a patient on the facts of his or her condition. Owning this truth constitutes the first step toward our healing, spiritual freedom, and wholeness. A revelation like this comes from love: God loves us just the way we are but too much to leave us that way.

Our own personal history of sin may be as obvious and as infamous as that of the prodigal son or the woman caught in adultery (Luke 15:11-24; John 8:2-11). It could be marked by sin that is more hidden and subtle, like that of a judgmental Pharisee or the brother of the prodigal son (Luke 7:36-50, esp. v. 39; Luke 15:25-32). It might be more glamorous, like that of a media star whose private life is scandalous. Perhaps it is like the head of a government who leads his or her people into an unjust war deemed patriotic but in truth is unjust. Whatever our history, we all are born into this human condition where we learn, especially from those closest to us, ways of relating that reinforce the sinful condition of the world.

The core energy and fundamental orientation of the human soul is toward God. We have all been made this way. But as noted earlier, something very early in human history skewed or damaged this holy, God-created "thirst and hunger for the Holy." Since then we have often "fed on food" other than the food God offers us. It has looked very good but does not satisfy or nourish us. We get drawn to what is self-inflating rather than to what is truthful, to what is self-pleasuring rather than self-sacrificing, to what promotes our status, reputation, and material comfort rather than believing in God and trusting in God's providence. Thus, the various distortions of our God-given energies of the soul are classically called the seven capital sins. More accurately, they refer to seven main tendencies of the human condition disposing us to sinful actions: pride, avarice or greed, lust, envy, anger, gluttony, and sloth. We experience their influence from within ourselves and from our cultural surroundings. These tendencies away from God impact our conscious and unconscious selves, shape our values and desires, affect our imagination and thinking, and, most importantly, influence the choices we make.

The remedy for this human condition is not some eradication or repression of these inclinations but, rather, a rechanneling of them. These energies of our soul were created by God, and created good. They need to be reclaimed, healed, and redirected toward the face of God. Such is the work of salvation throughout human history.

The study of addictions demonstrates how our souls naturally seek the Ultimate, the One we are calling Gracious Mystery; in fact, this yearning is precisely what most characterizes the soul.[5] Much of the history of the human family is filled with stories of many detours away from God, distractions, and even reversals along the way. We get attached or even addicted to various things or persons and invest in them all of our energy and hopes for fulfillment and salvation. So much of this drive for connecting with God is, in one sense, an all-consuming effort to escape what we most fear: namely, the possibility of our nothingness, of our being abandoned and left unloved. We long for a fullness that is possible only in a relationship with God. We long for belonging, for communion, to be loved and to love in return. Yet over and over again, like children easily stumbling and falling, we make bad choices.

In his excellent book *Addiction and Grace*[6] Gerald May claims that the most insidious and difficult-to-resist addiction is the temptation to believe that the perfect self is something we can achieve on our own. This could well be, under a different form, our effort to escape being abandoned and unloved. Like Saul, who through God's grace became Paul, we experience the self-defeating nature of this quest. We have to fail in order to "succeed." Otherwise, there will be no great unfolding; we will never pass over into God. Thankfully, by the grace of God there comes a day when we experience God's love and particularly God's accepting us as we are in this sinful state. Coming to this great awareness revolutionizes everything for us. We are freed to accept and love ourselves as we are in this state of powerlessness and great spiritual need.[7] We no longer have to cling to the "false god" of an idealized self that would be so perfect and lovable that we could never be abandoned or rejected. It sounds silly to think and act this way. Yet it "makes sense" for so much of the world in its manic search for security, affection, and esteem. As one who is the firstborn of a father who was the oldest male in his family of seven children and of a mother who was the oldest female in her family of nine, I can readily relate to May's point. I know from experience that such a quest ends in futility. It is to look for love, as the country song says, in all the wrong places.[8]

St. Ignatius of Loyola in his Spiritual Exercises guides the retreatant to consider this sobering fact of the human condition caught in sin and powerlessness. He has the person reflect on the story of the rebellious, fallen angels as one way to appreciate how this mystery of sin manifested itself even before humans were created. In this context he directs the person to recall the stories of the fallen angels and the original human beings in their fallen state, and then a hypothetical person who has seriously sinned and been lost forever. This meditation is meant to be powerful background for the retreatant leading to his or her experiencing embarrassment and sorrow for the manner in which all creation, including his or her own self, has responded so far to God's love. In addition, the retreatant will most likely feel a certain confusion or astonishment at the abiding love of God in the face of such insensitivity and ingratitude. To this end Ignatius has the retreatant come face to face with Jesus bleeding, thirsting, and struggling to breathe as he hangs on the cross, cruelly nailed there. Ignatius instructs the person to look intently at Jesus in such a state, lifted up for and because of him or her and every other human being, and then to ask three questions:

1. "What have I done for Christ?"

2. "What am I doing for Christ?"

3. In light of how he has loved me, "What ought I to do for Christ?"

Then Ignatius counsels the retreatant to talk with him as a friend would with a friend.[9]

Beginning a New Life

How overwhelming this can be for anyone giving himself or herself generously to these directives of St. Ignatius. The spiritual energy in such an encounter is the only power that can open the door of our heart to any hope of transforming this "bad news," the hard truth of our sinful state, into a story of Good News. Once we ask for the help of God's Spirit to open up to this love Christ has for us, this sad chapter in our life is transformed into Good News. Love triumphs over sin and death. It exposes sin for what it is, condemns it, and in Christ forgives and reconciles us.

God speaks unconditional love to us, as cited in chapter 1, but this time in a most unforgettable way. In his dying moments Jesus says, "Father, forgive them, for they know not what they do" (Luke 23:34)! This is not forgiveness extended to people who are simply weak in character. Instead, this is forgiveness given to those who cruelly calculated and manipulated justice while ignoring the commands of the covenant. To forgive what they did seems either foolishness of the worst kind . . . or it is divine love in its most amazing and creative sense. Such love overcomes all evils of the human family, in our own lives and in the lives of all other persons. It is more powerful than all the evils throughout all of human history, bar none. Is there anything as moving as this manifestation of mercy and compassion? When the human race was at its worst, God was at his best. No wonder Christians call the day on which this event happened Good Friday and not Bad Friday. Truly, it was the best of Fridays, the best of all days. Love is stronger than death and fear, hatred and revenge, war and racism, lust and greed. Thanks be to God that love has the last say in the human story! We can be filled with wonder as reflected in St. Bernard of Clairvaux's (d. 1153) words:

> In his first work [creation] he [God] gave me myself; in his second work [redemption] he gave me himself; when he gave me himself, he gave me back myself. Given, and regiven, I owe myself twice over. What can I give God in return for himself? Even if I could give him myself a thousand times, what am I to God?[10]

We Christians are so accustomed to looking at the crucifix and hearing the story of Jesus's death. We are familiar with the details of the story in which he forgives those who kill him. For many the power of this story rarely touches us much anymore, until maybe life thrusts us into a situation of powerlessness and vulnerability. Let me, then, tell what is essentially the same story but with very different circumstances. It is a story of the redeeming power of forgiveness and how mercy re-creates what was lost. We see how it transcends and even heals the deep alienation or separation of the human condition. It brings the self back into communion with its true self and brings the self into communion with the neighbor who had been wronged. Finally, through truth and love, it brings the self back into communion with God.

In an emotionally charged courtroom a South African woman stood listening to white police officers acknowledge their atrocities [before the Truth and Reconciliation Commission set up by the Nelson Mandela government of the 1990s to facilitate national healing following the terrible years of apartheid]. Officer van de Broek acknowledged that along with others, he had shot her 18 year old son at point-blank range. He and the others partied while they burned her son's body, turning it over and over on the fire until it was reduced to ashes.

Eight years later van de Broek and others returned to seize her husband. She was forced to watch her husband be bound to a woodpile, as they poured gasoline over his body and ignited the flames that consumed him. The last words she heard her husband say were: "Forgive them."

Now van de Broek awaited judgment. The Truth and Reconciliation Commission asked the woman what she wanted. "I want three things," she said calmly. "I want Mr. van de Broek to take me to the place where they burned my husband's body. I would like to gather up the dust and give him a decent burial. Second, Mr. van de Broek took all my family away from me, and I still have a lot of love to give. So twice a month I would like for him to come to the ghetto and spend a day with me so I can be a mother to him. Third, I would like Mr. van de Broek to know that he is forgiven by God and that I forgive him too. I would like to embrace him so he can know my forgiveness is real."

As the elderly woman was led across the courtroom, van de Broek fainted, overwhelmed. Someone began singing "Amazing Grace." Gradually everyone joined in.[11]

Only God and perhaps those who are well along in passing over into God could love and forgive in this way. We are all, deep down, Mr. van de Broek. We are all capable of the worst behavior and sometimes have even acted out such darkness, maybe many times.

At the same time, we are the South African woman. At least God is bringing us along this journey and is transforming us in some of the same amazing ways. We are being invited to a way of living free from fear, hatred, and the burden of harboring desires for revenge. This woman shows such a transformation can happen. God does such things, first by showing us the hard truth of our needing salvation from a frightful spiritual condition, and then showing us the overwhelming, wonderful possibility of our salvation. He offers to save us in his incomparable mercy and gives us his Heart, so that we might live as the South African woman was living—this divine way of living and loving.

Sin and grace: two sides of a single truth. The triumph of God's gracious love over sin and hopelessness is the greatest story ever told. We are the beneficiaries of such a gift if we accept it. What a destiny is ours! Such grace is what moved Jesus to say, "It is with desire that I have desired to eat this Passover with you before I suffer" (see Luke 22:15). It is as if he is saying, "I want to take you with me on this journey into God, into the Heart of my Abba so that you will know beyond any doubt that he is your Abba as well." This desire moved Jesus to tell the story of the homecoming of the prodigal son and the story of the finding of the hundredth sheep (Luke 15:1-7). It is what moved him to let the sinful, repentant woman celebrate her own coming home to God and to her true self by wiping with her hair his feet, wet from her tears (Luke 7:36-50). It moved Jesus to reach out to Zacchaeus, the tax collector, a role that made him in the eyes of his fellow Jews a traitor to the Romans (Luke 19:1-10). And this same desire is what moved Jesus to give the woman caught in adultery a future with God. He refused to condemn her, even though the scribes and Pharisees saw fit to define her only in terms of her past and felt justified in stoning her to death (John 8:2-11).

Paul Tillich, in his sermon cited earlier, speaks of the experience of God's grace in this situation of our fallen condition as the experience of being accepted for who we are and as we are in the moment. It is so often a great surprise to us when this grace or blessing comes; it is completely unmerited and by no means implies that we are thereby freed from our sins. It moves St. Paul to exclaim, "Where sin abounds, there grace abounds all the more!" (Rom 5:20). Tillich goes on to say that grace comes to us in those situations when we are going through dark times of meaninglessness and failure, or when we are in terrible pain and restlessness of soul, or when our efforts over many years to be perfect prove to be still fruitless, or when despair has destroyed all our joy and courage. Grace comes to us in such a variety of ways, as it did in dramatic fashion to Saul (Acts 9:1-22) and the future apostle Matthew (Matt 9:9-13). In his essay-sermon "You Are Accepted," Tillich depicts Grace (God) saying with love and strong assurance, "You are accepted, accepted by that which is Love and greater than you, the name of which you do not know." This is the blessing that overcomes the separation burdening us deep inside, as it does all other human beings since our beginnings. It is the Good News of the Gospel. This grace takes the word of God first spoken to us as unconditional love and makes it much deeper and more significant for us than in that first encounter. Now we know that this Gracious Mystery of love knows our dark secrets, our fears and shame and guilt, and is not put off by them but is moved to mercy. If we say yes, we are then freed from the need to hide, to live in fear and with pretense. We feel the invitation and courage to treat ourselves like God does. We can come out in the open and live in the freedom this love offers. It is our great exodus, our being liberated from spiritual death, released for new life with God.

The Turning Point of Our Journey: Believing or Not

The core of all our sins, then, is our not believing that we are loved or even lovable. It expresses itself largely in our not trusting this new surprising, unmerited gift of Divine Love. We do not want to depend on it or live in relationship with it but, rather, we choose to trust in our own self-made selves, in our own accomplishments and successes, ultimately in our own experiences. This was the original sin of the angels, the original sin of the first humans and the same for each one of us. We want in one way or another "to do it my way," to escape our finitude, to be independent and self-sufficient as much as possible. Implicitly we want to be God by being in control of our lives. In choosing to live this way, however, we imitate the three-year-old girl not wanting to come out from behind her daddy's legs.

The core of all of our graces, then, is our being loved by God unconditionally. It offers us all we need for living in peace and with courage to trust that we walk with love in every present moment. It shows us the foolishness, futility, and loneliness of trying to live a lifestyle of self-sufficiency, of trusting ultimately in our own selves. Eventually, grace will catch up with anyone who tries to live a life that ignores God. Grace leads us to acknowledge our humanity, to accept ourselves as accepted, forgiven, and loved by God. It empowers us to choose to live in fidelity to this newly discovered true self and then to experience our spirits unfolding, opening up in joy and gratitude to the One who first loved us. Once we have the courage to open up to these wonderful blessings, there comes out of us, so naturally and powerfully, the desire to make a return of this love, in some way or other. This is a very important moment in our Passover journey into God, a major turning point from self-centered living to the beginning of living for a great love that is our new center. We now wait for a word, for some kind of direction from this Gracious Mystery. We are moved to say something like, "You have so loved me. In your tender mercies you have given me another chance. You have even given me the best you have to give, your own Son who gave his life for me. How might I love you back? I have never been loved before like you have loved me. I have never before met anyone like you! Whatever you wish, I am at your disposal. Anything you want, you have it. So speak, Lord, your servant is listening."

In this offering, then, we are witnessing a great freeing in our lives: freedom from fear and various forms of sin and also freedom for our true selves to live out of love and hope. God's way of relating is being formed in our own spirits. There is a new disposition emerging in us of wanting to offer ourselves, eventually even to give away ourselves, just like God does in Jesus. These new developments are a sure sign of the Holy Spirit's miracle of re-creating us. What is fascinating is to see what God's Spirit does with these new desires emerging in us. This is what we will consider in the following chapter.

Questions for Discussion and Faith-Sharing

1. When have you experienced this mystery of being accepted and loved as you are? What was that like?

2. Have you experienced the desire, maybe even the longing, to give away—out of love—your own self? In what ways and situations has this happened?

3. What is the fundamental, core temptation for you: to control life or hide from it? What particular ways has it been expressed in your life? What motives, thoughts, and emotions are part of this kind of experience?

4. When in your life did God become personal for you; when did God become Someone who knows and loves you and was no longer an impersonal, distant lawgiver or threat?

5. Find on the internet or elsewhere a reproduction of Rembrandt's painting of the return of the prodigal son. Ponder it closely, study the main characters in it, take time to identify with each of them, and share the feelings and

thoughts, the desires and hopes that arise inside you. Henri Nouwen's *The Return of the Prodigal Son* is a wonderful source for praying with this theme of repentance, reconciliation, and healing.

Chapter Three

CALLED AND SENT

It is inspiring to witness individuals who are loved and at the same time flawed, yet nonetheless are forgiven and accepted for who they are. What can be more inspiring is to witness them, after being so blessed, giving themselves generously and tirelessly to others or to a great cause or project. As a teacher I have experienced such moments when I see, despite their problems and immaturity, the dedication and excitement of some students regarding their future. Then there are parents who are greatly moved and feel so rewarded to see their children overcome limits and earlier mistakes and achieve some great success in their profession or life. And it can be quite touching and even a glimpse of God to watch what happens when people fall in love with each other. We see beauty and goodness in them, deeper and stronger than their shortcomings, and rejoice at how they come to new life thanks to this newly discovered love. Such examples give us a sense of the state of soul of the person described at the end of the last chapter.

How wonderful when that person is one's very own self. When we allow ourselves to be forgiven and embraced with a tender acceptance and gracious welcome, we experience ourselves as never before. We are freed from many negative things, especially the temptation to self-rejection, thanks to the mercy and kindness of God. We experience ourselves ushered into a new way of being. For some it is so profound that it is like coming back from the dead.

We are now disposed to take the next major step in our Passover journey into God. Filled with gratitude, joy, and praise, we are inspired to offer ourselves back to the One who first loved us and like no other. We find something of the desires of Jesus in our hearts, when he said in his last hours, "It is with desire that I have desired to eat this Passover with you" (see Luke 22:15). What is emerging from our depths are the longings of God for communion and lasting relationship promised in the covenant. These new desires of ours echo God's Heart and manifest the beginnings of our being transformed as a new creation in Christ.

Being Called

This, then, is the setting in which God takes us up on the offering of ourselves, and God does this by giving us another gift. He gives us a call that opens up our life to new meaning and purpose. God's call is an invitation to live a shared life with Jesus in work and in friendship. It is to discover who we are by accepting this divine invitation to make the mission of Jesus our own mission and the ultimate purpose of our life.

What, then, is this mission that God gave to Jesus who, in turn, gives to each and every one of us? It is to bring forth the kingdom or reign of God in time and space. This is the great work of God throughout history. So central is this biblical image of the kingdom of God in the teachings of Jesus that one can confidently assert that the meaning and value of anyone's life depends on how he or she relates to it. The kingdom of God expresses the Source of all that is and ever will be, namely, Gracious Mystery who is present to each and all of us in the relationships and ordinariness of our day. Whether our life is largely that of making a good marriage and raising children with all of its challenges; or if it is, rather, a life in the public arena given to health care or politics, legal or financial services, manufacturing or law enforcement, transportation or farming, social work or psychological therapy, ordained ministry or the arts, it finds its ultimate meaning and purpose in relation to this overarching reality of the kingdom of God. Whatever we do with our life at any moment either enhances or inhibits the coming of this gift. It is what makes the ordinariness of our lives extraordinary. What a difference it makes in our life when we can see with faith this divine, Gracious Mystery in and around us, sustaining and giving love and direction to all that makes up our life and all of creation around us.

St. Gregory the Great (d. 604) says this about the kingdom: "The kingdom of God has no assessment value put on it, but it is worth everything you have. To Zacchaeus it was worth half his goods, because he kept the other half to restore fourfold what he had taken unjustly; to Peter and Andrew it was worth the nets and boat they gave up; to the widow it was worth two small coins [all she had]; to another person it was worth a cup of cold water. The kingdom of God, as I said, is worth everything you have."[1]

What more precisely, then, is this kingdom or reign of God? What does it look like, or how does one speak about it? We need to reflect on this at some length in order to appreciate the nature and importance of God's calling and sending us. It is foundational for everything that follows.

The Kingdom of God

Curiously enough, Jesus never gives a definition of the kingdom. This frustrates some Westerners who like clear and distinct ideas, sometimes with mathematical or scientific clarity in whatever they are discussing or studying. This is not, however, the way people from Jesus's time and culture (Semitic/Arabic) would think or speak; instead, he gives us stories and images of the kingdom to ponder; he offers us an intuitive understanding of this reality, which is much more of the realm of mystery than something like a specific object we can measure, weigh, or define.

Jesus much preferred to say the kingdom of God is like this or that: like a mustard seed growing up into a large bush, or like yeast rising up in bread dough. It is like the Good Samaritan, a foreigner considered to be religiously unacceptable, perhaps even evil, who graces us with surprisingly generous acts of compassionate love and healing. It is like the father of the prodigal son who restores into his graces the wayward, profligate son and offers the same generous welcome to the other son paralyzed with envy and resentment because of the father's kindness and forgiveness shown to his brother. It is like the man who plans a big dinner and invites a large number of guests who decline the invitation with one excuse or another. The man, angered by their responses, orders his servants to bring in the poor and crippled, the lame and blind, and even after that, to compel people of any kind to come so that his house will be filled. Again, the kingdom of God is like the merchant in search of fine pearls; upon finding one pearl of great price, he proceeds to sell all he has in order to buy it. Lastly, the kingdom is compared to a large net thrown into the sea. When workers haul in the net filled with all kinds of fish, they sort out the good from the bad.

What these parables and stories offer is a picture of the kingdom as a great gift, freely and generously given. It comes upon us as a surprise and often with notable impact in our life. It manifests an attitude of great self-sacrifice, of forgiveness and reconciliation, of joy and at the same time an expectation of some kind of positive response and change of one's ways. Jesus is pointing to the kingdom as God's active and powerful presence, bringing with it a great promise of something yet to come but already happening in the present moment. Its distinctive sign is tender, reconciling love and mercy, rather than judgment and punishment. The very essence of all the demonstrated images in these parables is a divine Love "so powerful that it pushed Him [God] to the point of insanity. . . . [God] dispenses with the normal canons of discretion and good taste in dealing with us. . . . The trouble with the God that Jesus . . . represents is that He loves too much."[2] Jesus hanging on the cross, nailed there for each of us, is the human realization of this kingdom and of a God who loves us unto folly. It is, as Gregory the Great says, worth everything you have.

The kingdom, then, is a reality that upsets many social habits and accepted ways of being. It continues to challenge, from Jesus's day to our own, the comfort level of many. It prompts us to associate with the so-called undesirables and religiously unfit. Jesus said, "I choose to be with such people because they are sick and need me, because they are truly repentant, and they feel the gratitude of children forgiven by God . . . above all, because I know what God is like, so good to the poor, so glad when the lost are found, so overflowing with a father's love for the returning child, so merciful to the despairing, the helpless, the needy. That is why [I associate with such kind]!"[3] Anyone embracing this vision of the kingdom and its gracious spirit would do the same.

It can also be said that the kingdom is a Presence whose love will have the last say. Its triumph is inevitable. This is why Jesus could speak of the mission his Father gave him as a mission with an assured outcome. His love will prevail! It is impossible to avoid this divine Presence or stop it or even kill it.[4]

The Freedom Given in the Kingdom

And so this Gracious Mystery of ever-giving love invites all of us to live each day of the rest of our lives with an indomitable hope in the midst of all we do. Even times of trial and suffering, sadness and temptation are undergirded with the blessed assurance of the One who has loved so much. Thus, this Gracious Mystery, living in our depths, becomes our anchor, our refuge, and our rock in whom we trust. Because of this deep-down Mystery of goodness, we trust life and its overall direction and eventual outcome. We have discovered the One who is in love with life and will go to any length to save it, heal it, restore it, transform it, and share with it even Divinity. We have come to believe in the One who loved us and gave himself up for us. Death is powerless in the face of it. How could we not choose to give ourselves to such a unique, gracious Reality and mission?

When we truly believe and are grounded in this life-changing, world-changing Reality, we are freed from the distractions of various worries and anxieties. We are freed from the attachments to substitute gods that commonly weigh people down and prevent significant spiritual growth. Our focus, then, will be on what Jesus declares to be "the one thing necessary,"[5] whose love and promise of eternal life now and forever center us and guide us in all we do and have to endure. We grow into a way of living that the Jewish scribes described as "liv[ing] now as though God reigned and no-one else had any power over you." We find in Jesus the supreme model of this spiritual freedom, since "his attitude relativizes and diminishes, one might say dwarfs, the power of those who can kill the body, but cannot touch spirit or purpose or vision." As we journey into the fulfillment of this great promise of the kingdom, we realize in our own life, even now, something of the amazing balance and depth of Jesus's freedom: "his quiet confidence, his ready and immense compassion for any kind of suffering, the utter simplicity of his approach to life and people and theological or ethical problems, and his deep and spontaneous piety."[6] Transformation in God is truly happening to us. We are journeying into God.

The kingdom of God refers to God's active, loving, invitational presence in our lives but also to the effects or impact of that mysterious presence in human relations. One example is living as though God now reigns and no one has any power over us, as mentioned above. Another example: just as yeast raises bread dough, this Presence gives rise to human communities that embody this Presence and so are called, in a derivative sense, the kingdom of God. Father Joachim Jeremias in his *New Testament Theology* presents an extensive description of what life looks like for such individuals and communities who receive this gift of God's loving invitation and presence as they journey to God. It is a glimpse of what can happen in spirit and body for people, married and single, families and religious communities, work environments, schools, parishes, cities, and nations.

Traits of the Kingdom

Jeremias cites the following traits of those who give clear signs of the presence of God and how their way of being together in work and leisure can be called the kingdom of God . . . or at least an instance of its manifestation.

1. Above all, having an indefatigable capacity to forgive others; the kind of community whose members have experienced forgiveness; out of gratitude, its members extend to others the same favor they have been shown; the most Godlike trait in the kingdom

2. Wishing peace to all

3. Self-effacing in public, not seeking honor and applause

4. Being careful in speech; always truthful, never slandering nor condemning others nor creating suspicion; no oath taking but being simple in saying yes or no

5. Giving of possessions; God is truly the God of one's heart; "mammonism" is out; security, meaning, and hope are not possessions but in Abba Father and the salvation of Jesus, the pearl of inestimable price; ready and willing to share with those in need

6. Showing respect and love to woman for her own sake and not as a sex object; Jesus brings woman out of seclusion, hidden by Jewish society because of fear that sexual desire was uncontrollable

7. Relating to children as priceless in value, where Jewish society in its legal system saw them, like women, of much less value than men

8. Avoiding narrow nationalism, fostering of rebellion and violence, particularism in politics

9. Subordinating work to the seeking of the kingdom, God's reign in our hearts and communities, which implies there is good work and bad work[7]

Jeremias is not giving a complete list but rather a number of symptoms or examples of what happens when the kingdom of God, this Sacred Presence or Gracious Mystery, is allowed to break into our world even while residing under the power of sin, death, and the devil. Furthermore, God's kingdom lays claim to our whole life. The disciples of Jesus, then, are to look for manifestations of this Spirit in every aspect of life. Our whole life is to witness to the world that the kingdom or reign of God has dawned, that this amazing divine Presence is acting now in the midst of our daily lives. We are called to do this, not on our own, but with Jesus the Christ, the Lord of this new way of being and living. We are invited to share with him in the work this involves and in the wonderful companionship that flows from it.

A Meditation on the Kingdom

Ignatius of Loyola in his Spiritual Exercises facilitates the process by which we respond to this invitation by posing a scene for us to meditate. We are to imagine a human king, clearly a man of

God and one whom people respect and obey. The king invites as many as possible to join him in a great cause, "to conquer all the land of unbelievers"[8] and be content to share with him in everything it involves: food, drink, and dress, successes and struggles, victories and labors. Finally, we are to consider how a good person ought to respond to such a kind and generous offer and how "mean-spirited" one would be not to respond positively to such a worthy king.

Most guides of the Spiritual Exercises today adapt this scene by having the person imagine a much admired contemporary or more recent leader inviting him or her, as well as others, to a great and worthy cause. This makes Ignatius's consideration more interesting and engaging for the prayer of contemporary retreatants. Examples of such leaders could be Mother Teresa of Calcutta, Dorothy Day, Abraham Lincoln, Mahatma Gandhi, William Wilberforce, Nelson Mandela, or Martin Luther King Jr. How honored one would be to be invited by any one of these to their famous work or efforts.

Once we decide on what our response would be to one of these great leaders, Ignatius has us apply his parable to Christ. We are to imagine Jesus Christ, the King of all kings as Ignatius calls him, issuing a call to us to join him in "conquer[ing] all the world and all enemies and so enter into the glory of my Father. Therefore whoever would like to come with me is to labor with me, that following me in the pain, he [or she] may also follow me in the glory."[9] Ignatius assumes that the person engaging in this exercise would be greatly honored and complimented to receive a call to the work of such a great leader. He anticipates that this person is well disposed to make an even more generous response to Christ and his invitation. Ignatius finishes by having the person reflect on how anyone with good judgment and reason would gladly offer his or her entire self to this invitation and work, an invitation from none other than Christ himself, and with victory assured.

The meditation concludes with a remarkable prayer Ignatius composed. We are encouraged to pray it to Jesus, "The Eternal

King and Lord of All,"[10] as a friend would speak to a friend. In it we offer not only our whole selves for this mission but go further and promise to act against anything in ourselves that would make our response less than total. According to St. Ignatius, we would "make offerings of greater value and greater importance." At this climactic point Ignatius has us make a great leap of love and daring trust by asking Christ, in the presence of the Mother of God and all the other saints, to be given the grace to imitate him in "bearing all injuries and all abuse, and all poverty of spirit and actual [physical] poverty, too,"[11] but only if Jesus would choose us for this and that it would bring greater service and praise to God.

When we first come upon this prayer, we may be left wary or even breathless, overwhelmed possibly because of the vulnerability to which it exposes us. But at this stage of the journey, at least in the scheme of Ignatius, it is hoped that we will see the prayer as an ideal into which we will want to grow. We will desire to have such desires someday and, if it is God's call that would give greater love and service to God, we will even realize some of these desires in our lives. We are to ask to be "ready and diligent"[12] to respond to whatever the call and particular shape or form it might take. Ignatius hopes we will begin to sense that someday, with a special love that lifts us beyond any fear of what this might cost, we will love God unto folly, just as God has loved us already in Christ . . . unto folly. What Ignatius's prayer reflects, then, is radical living and radical loving expressive of the logic of love. It is a way of relating to God, to Gracious Mystery that characterizes the triune God's life of not just mutuality in relations but total mutuality, the complete giving of one's self to the other and the complete receiving of the other in the total giving of one's own self. In its human expression, it is to love as Jesus the Christ loved the Father and us, completely poured out.

Sometime during this Passover journey into God, we must embrace such desires as expressive of the depths of our own souls. To become who we are destined to become in God, we have to identify with Jesus in his sayings, "This is my Body, my whole self, given up for you" and "It is with desire that I have desired to eat this Passover with you before I suffer." At least, we need to eventually identify with such longings if we are to become fully who we are. This prayer in response to the invitation of Jesus, then, is the first hint of the life for which God has destined us. It is something that is far more than we could have ever imagined yet is shown to us in Christ crucified and risen, the firstborn of a whole new creation, a new world in God we are destined for someday.

The book of Ruth in the Hebrew Scriptures is a beautiful anticipation of this call of Christ and radical response to the call. Ruth, a Gentile, leaves her people, land, religion, and culture to marry an Israelite, a son of the covenant, and then stays with all of these choices, completely giving herself, even after she is widowed early in her marriage. A thousand years before Christ, she shows us the spirit and extraordinary love of a disciple of Christ for Christ.

Then in St. John's gospel, chapter 21, there is the threefold reply of Peter, the apostle, to the risen Christ, who asks him three times whether he loves him, and loves him more than he loves the others. Each time Peter says he loves the Lord and each time the risen Lord sends him to feed his lambs and sheep. Jesus predicts Peter's total outpouring later in a crucifixion that will mark the end of his life. Peter will become an image of the God who loves unto folly.

There is also the powerful testimony of St. Paul in chapter 3 of his Letter to the Philippians in which he expresses himself with his usual intensity. He says there that he has come to re-evaluate everything since encountering Christ. So much of what he formerly considered to be of supreme value he has now come to think of as "rubbish"! Encountering the risen Christ has changed his entire world. This has engendered in his heart longings to continue his pursuit of "perfect maturity" in Christ. He hoped someday that all would be given to him by the One who raised Christ from the dead.

We are left, then, to give our own answer to this call. We might be at the beginning of our adult lives ready to make a choice that will deeply affect the way we live the rest of our lives. It could be our answer to a marriage proposal or what we do with inner stirrings to join a religious community or a seminary. It could be a decision in favor of a long preparation for a career and vocation in education, medicine, law, politics, or one of the arts. It might be a midlife response or even a later awakening to this Sacred Presence: making a choice within the context of an already life-shaping choice made at a younger age. Or it can be a new attitude and deeper commitment to what we have already been doing with our lives but chosen this time for motives much more informed by a deep encounter with Christ. Really meeting him, maybe for the first time, will open us to a much deeper appreciation of the value and great consequences our choices make on others and the whole world. These can be major choices, but they can also be more hidden, hardly noticeable choices that only God sees. Even these humble ones can embody a love and gratitude for life much deeper than what we were formerly capable of bringing to our actions in earlier days. What comes to mind as an example is the parent who many times sets aside his or her preference or convenience to be available to his or her children in need. The call of Christ can be there many times during a day.

What matters is the depth of gratitude and love we bring, thanks to God's Holy Spirit, to whatever we do or undergo, regardless of how inconsequential the world judges its value. Whenever we draw such spiritual depth from our communion with Christ and bring it to whatever we do, there is unleashed a power or energy that is nothing less than godly. It contributes to what the Hebrew prophets and St. Paul call co-creation with God, the Creator. God takes our faith and love, in whatever we do or undergo, and uses them in bringing some part of our world to a newer state—healing it, guiding it, inspiring it, opening it up to some new possibilities in Christ. The kingdom of God is made more manifest. In partnership with Christ, then, our life helps in the further unfolding of this one universal reality, the kingdom or reign of God.

Personal Examples

I have experienced a call from Christ in major ways on a number of occasions. As I look back to the time when I was only nine years old I recall the desires that were in my heart to be a Jesuit and priest someday. I enjoyed being a server at the Masses of our family's parish community, and this provided me a friendly ambiance for opening up to this vocational possibility. Then when I was nineteen years old and in the second year of college engineering, I made a weekend retreat the university mandated for its Catholic students. This brought to a climax the life-direction question that had gone "below my consciousness" during my earlier teens. It became clear to me that I had to enter the Jesuits to seek a sense of confirmation of what I discerned to be my call. I was "following my bliss," acting on a strong sense of direction in my spirit that had come upon me that weekend. If I had read my soul incorrectly, then I could always leave the Jesuits. But not to have acted on this encounter would, I sensed, do significant harm to my soul. Act I must, and so I did.

Then in another setting: for many years as a Jesuit seminarian and young priest I experienced the call of Christ numerous times as I made various decisions regarding the course of studies in which I was engaging. These were choices made in relation to my preparing for teaching university students someday. At the same time my father was dying and I had to make time to listen to the insights and inspirations of Christ's Spirit as I prepared for and led his funeral.

But there was no call that cost as much and engaged me as much as a time during my forties when I fell in love with a woman close to my own age. This challenged everything in my depths, even my sense of having correctly discerned years ago my life as a Jesuit and priest. For some time this experience moved in my consciousness, usually in a gentle fashion, but eventually it built toward a demand for a clear yes or no. I engaged for quite some time in extra prayer and psychological therapy to know my truth. In my forty-eighth year I lived in limbo for some five months while not knowing my truth and not knowing what answer to give. It seemed I no longer knew who I was or what I was to do with the rest of my life. Then one day in the midst of some anguished exchange between God and myself, I said, "It does not matter to me whether I am a priest or a married man. What does matter is that I am with you and your Christ. Christ Jesus is the most precious gift I have ever received in my whole life and I am nothing and utterly lost if disconnected from him. Please . . . don't ever let that happen!" A few days later I knew myself with a new clarity, and I experienced Christ and God at a depth I had never known before. It was like I had awakened from a long sleep. The darkness of those five months and the ongoing questioning of the previous years were over and now I could assume my role in life with a new sense of who I am and how I could best live in fidelity to this truth. I was ready to make choices coming from a freedom I had not experienced before.

How this all made me appreciate something of what those who contemplate divorce go through, whether they choose to stay or leave! To be able to hear and act on the call to our truth and to deeper relationship with Christ is an enormous gift. To know who we are and to be free to act on it is such a gift. That affirmation and call is the cornerstone of the spiritual building God is erecting in us.

But more important than being called to work in helping the kingdom of God come, we are called to companionship, to friendship with Christ Jesus himself. We are called to rejoice in and savor the gift of this divine Gift-giver. Before we do anything at all in the name of the kingdom of God, we are meant to appreciate that this personal God has given himself to us, that we are precious in his eyes, called and known by name, and loved for who we are. To heed this wisdom is to open ourselves to incredible spiritual strength for the work that will follow. The Christian Liturgy of the Word continuously proclaims this fundamental truth. It reminds us over and over again about who we are to God and to Christ, and that it is from this holy connection with the Divine that we are sent to share in the mission of Jesus as we live our lives with him each day of it.

As our lives go on we hopefully come to appreciate a universal truth: that for all the good and kind things we might do for others in response to Christ's call, the most important part of our mission and what has the most lasting impact is our reflecting back to others their God-given goodness and how deeply God loves them. It is to help them know this great love and how welcomed, accepted, and forgiven they are. They need not be anxious or afraid. Is this not what Jesus did? Was this not the centerpiece of his mission, to lead them to Abba? We may be the type of person who rarely, if ever, verbalizes this to others, but hopefully our actions speak it.

An Obstacle to Living Our Call

The following saying has resonated profoundly with me and so many seekers of the truth of their lives. It speaks directly to that part of our being where we might fear living our call and succumb to the temptation to hide ourselves and our gifts under a bushel basket. We need encouragement to trust this marvelous gift of our person and the divine call to open up to a rich and beautiful life with Jesus and Abba, full of meaning and priceless relationships.

> Our deepest fear is not that we are inadequate. Our deepest fear is that we are powerful beyond measure. It is our light, not our darkness that most frightens us. We ask ourselves, Who am I to be brilliant, gorgeous, talented, fabulous? Actually, who are

you *not* to be? You are a child of God. Your playing small does not serve the world. There is nothing enlightened about shrinking so that other people won't feel insecure around you. . . . We were born to make manifest the glory of God that is within us. It's not just in some of us; it's in everyone. And as we let our own light shine, we unconsciously give other people permission to do the same. As we are liberated from our own fear, our presence automatically liberates others.[13]

So often Jesus says in the gospels, "Fear is useless. What you need is faith." This is what St. Ignatius encourages anyone making the Spiritual Exercises to ask for: a freedom from anything that would make him or her "deaf to [Christ's] call," but rather, to be "ready and diligent to fulfill His most holy will."[14]

So the question is, What is it that will heal our fears and move us to courage of soul, to trust this call and live with generosity of heart? What will empower us to go forth with faith and love? This is the question the next chapter addresses.

Questions for Discussion and Faith-Sharing

1. Do you see your life as a response to a calling from God and/or Christ? How so?

2. Name some ways in which your life now helps to bring forth the kingdom of God.

3. Which of the traits of the kingdom cited by Joachim Jeremias in this chapter surprise you? Can you add to this list?

4. Find on the internet or elsewhere a copy of the painting *The Annunciation* by Henry Ossawa Tanner. Look closely at the face of Mary, her eyes and hands also; hear her say, "How can this be?" Can you identify with her experience in your own life? How so?

5. Ponder and pray on a copy of Caravaggio's painting of the call of Levi the tax collector and future apostle Matthew. Note the finger of Christ when pointing to Levi and how similar it is to God's finger reaching out to Adam in Michelangelo's fresco of the creation. See also Caravaggio's painting of Saul at the moment of his calling—how he is knocked to the ground and blinded by the light of Jesus whom he was persecuting.

Chapter Four

ENLIGHTENED AND EMPOWERED

Imagine yourself being able to fly, in an instant, from one place in the world to any other place. Imagine visiting a home and observing from a hidden place a painful conversation between a conflicted husband and wife. Accusations and bitter denials follow regarding the husband's extramarital affair. Jealousy, anger, and threats of divorce and retaliation are voiced. The couple's children are awakened and peek in from their bedrooms while observing with fright their parents tearing at each other.

Then you move on to a boardroom filled with political and military leaders of a nation engaged in a bitterly fought war. You overhear words of hatred and the desire for revenge as plans are made for a surprise nighttime bombing attack on an unsuspecting city of the enemy. Thousands of noncombatants will be incinerated. The pain of the survivors will be horrible.

Next, you come to a hospital emergency ward. An elderly, alcohol-reeking woman, mugged and found at the curb of a backstreet of the city, has just been picked up by an ambulance and brought in for critical care. You hear her tell a sad story of neglect and abandonment: no relatives or friends to care for her, minimal financial resources, only sorrow and woe.

Lastly, you witness a courtroom scene in which a male teacher of high school students is on trial for alleged sexual improprieties with a high school girl. The girl was embarrassed and strongly resentful of this teacher's confronting her about her attempt to cheat on a very important exam. She had wanted to maximize her chances of being admitted into the university of her choice; doing well on this exam was crucial to that hope. Being so humiliated by this situation and also pressured by her parents to succeed in her studies, the girl falsely accuses the teacher. Even if he is proven innocent, the teacher's trustworthiness in respecting boundaries will forever be suspect in the minds of some.

How heavy these scenes are, how unsettling to visualize one after the other. They are examples, however, that illustrate rather well what Ignatius of Loyola wants a person making the contemplation on the annunciation and incarnation of Christ in the Spiritual Exercises to imagine and ponder: the triune God looking down from the heavens at a world without God's presence. They are glimpses of a world lost and disconnected from God and moving toward a hell of its own making. Such a "view from above," however, does not prompt divine rejection and condemnation but, rather, compassion and an amazing, completely unexpected intervention. Furthermore, instead of standing on the outside of our human situation and helping only from a distance, God in great humility does what is a total surprise by stepping into this situation: becoming human in Jesus. Jesus is the help that the triune God sends us. In him the Divine becomes human; Divinity joins humanity. This is an event unprecedented in human history. In Jesus the Christ Gracious Mystery reverses the crisis in human relationships and history. In Jesus God becomes one of us to experience all that we experience: feeling what we feel, learning as we have to learn, suffering and rejoicing, hoping and praying as we do. In doing this he transforms humanity, saving it from hopelessness and death. This is the mission given to Jesus.

Our own mission and life purpose is to have some active part in this same mission given to Jesus. We may have been engaged for some years in a life work, but we usually do not hear the call of Christ in it and realize what our share is in his mission until we begin to know him fairly well. To know and love him opens up our understanding to the deeper meaning of our life and its work. Knowing him as living now heals us of our fears, gives us courage, and moves us to trust his call to serve and offer ourselves with generosity. More and more we become free in this living, growing relationship and trust him to send us wherever we can serve best the work of the kingdom.

Meeting Jesus

Who, then, is Jesus? And how do we come to the kind of personal knowledge and love of him that grounds our call and gives courage to offer ourselves in service for building the kingdom or reign of God? Jesus is so many things according to the Scriptures: bread for the world, Light of the World, the Word of God, Son of David, Son of Man, Lord and Savior, the Good Shepherd, Teacher, Messiah, healer, exorcist, and so on.

Before all of these, however, he is Son and deepest delight of God. He experienced himself in this beautiful and tender way, especially during his time at the Jordan River when he participated in a ritual John the Baptist conducted for sinners wanting to repent and be spiritually cleansed. Jesus, the sinless One, yet wanting to identify with sinners, freely put himself in this ritual before the One he called Abba. He offered himself completely and humbly at this beginning of his public ministry. As he came up out of the water he had a profound experience of God affirming him as "my beloved Son, with whom I am well pleased" (Matt 3:17). This moment would become the foundation piece of his relationship with God and all he did in the name of God.

It would be the basis of his revealing God as tender and compassionate like a wonderful Abba, rather than someone distant and having to be feared and placated. This personal knowledge and love of God would be fully embraced by the human Jesus after what would soon follow his experience at the Jordan River.

Jesus, Tested in the Desert

The Spirit of God led Jesus into the desert to spend forty days there praying, fasting, and being exposed to three temptations. One was an appeal to find his security in material things: "If you are the Son [Beloved] of God, command that these stones become loaves of bread." A second was an appeal to fame and esteem, implying the people will be in awe of Jesus's superhuman ways and do his least wish: "If you are the Son [Beloved] of God, throw yourself down" from the pinnacle of the Jerusalem temple. "He [God] will command his angels . . . with their hands they will support you, lest you dash your foot against a stone." The third temptation was an offer of power and the control of empires throughout the world in all their magnificence: "All these I shall give to you, if you will prostrate yourself and worship me" (Matt 4:3, 5, 9).

Together, these three temptations constitute one basic temptation, namely, to doubt or simply forget the Father's affirmation—"This is my beloved Son, with whom I am well pleased"—and to trust in his own achievements. If Jesus trusted this tempting voice, he would then work diligently to establish his own self-worth and try to make himself secure and lovable. This bears a striking resemblance to the temptations that the angels, the first human beings, and any one of us have often succumbed to in one form or another. How often do we in little ways and sometimes in a big way find ourselves dissatisfied with who we are and therefore prone to envy and feelings of inferiority? We want to be bigger than life, like a god in a way, at least not so limited or too ordinary, while we look for a love that ironically has already been offered us again and again. Jesus, like all human beings, was exposed to voices of contradiction and fear that counseled anxiety about the future and the need to trust in his own self and make his way on his own. Such voices challenged, even contradicted the voice of God spoken at the Jordan River. It was as if this inner voice of temptation were saying, "Oh, you are not the beloved Son pleasing to the Father, but I will tell you how you can make that happen. Change these stones to bread, that is, be the kind of Messiah who provides the bread or material needs of the people and then they will surely follow you. Second, throw yourself from the pinnacle of the temple, that is, stop identifying with human beings and being so limited. Use your Divinity to charm them into following God and God's covenant. Third, and finally, fall down and worship me, that is, you can have so much power to lead these people to freedom and social order, first by being king or governor of a nation liberated from the Romans and then after that, who knows, perhaps the whole world." All in all, this insidious voice counsels Jesus to trust in his own self rather than in God, his Abba. Through fear, lying, and exaggeration it tries to foster doubt about God's affirmation and confuse Jesus about who he is. But thanks to his knowing the Father so intimately, Jesus sees through these deceptions and quotes from Scripture to rebut each of them.

It is important to note that in countering these three temptations Jesus embraced more deeply than before the relationship he enjoyed with God. He chose not to take counsel through the empty lies of Satan but to trust the Father he had known since his childhood (Luke 2:41-50, esp. v. 49). He held in memory and trusted the powerful affirmation he recently received during his baptism at the Jordan River. Because this event has enormous implications for our own Passover into God, it is very important to note that Jesus chose to trust his true self, his self connected to Abba, when trusting God and God's love for him. Herein would be found the clue to Jesus's life and ministry being so powerful, truly salvific and transforming of human beings and societies. His choice hints at the transforming possibilities for our own journey and with whatever we do in our life to help bring forth God's kingdom.

Wellsprings of Jesus's Ministry

What is revealed in this choice right up to his dying moments is the core of his being. He knows he is not his own person in the sense of a Western, highly individualized self. Rather, he is ever aware of being part of a relationship, part of a "we," and it is the Spirit of his Abba Father who is the other person in this mysterious reality. This, then, is who he is: One who belongs, who is Son, beloved, and accompanied. This relationship describes his identity, his true self. He is only to the degree he is present to and lives in fidelity to the One with whom he shares this holy union. From the Spirit Jesus is blessed with guidance, knowledge, and love. It is because Jesus spoke and acted in communion with this divine Source in his depths that his teachings, preaching, and healings were so acclaimed by the people of his day. To the dismay of many of the official leaders of Judaism at that time, the people would exclaim how different his words were from those of the scribes and Pharisees. They remarked that he acted with authority and power, something they were not witnessing in their religious leaders. The gospels of Matthew, Mark, and Luke speak of Jesus acting with a certain *exousia*, translated as "authority" but meaning far more than what the word authority usually communicates in English.[1] People were hearing God and God's depths when Jesus preached or taught. His deeds reflected a power or *dunamis*[2] that they knew could come only from God. It was obvious to them that his mission was "authored" by God, grounded or rooted in God's Spirit, not as some of the Pharisees said, in the devil or Beelzebul (see Luke 11:15, 18). All that Jesus did, whether his praying, his discerning, or anything he spoke or acted on, were empowered from that sacred place in himself where he and the Father live in deepest communion.

Claiming This Same Inner Power

As was said earlier, this deepest reality in Jesus is Good News for us. That is because this same relational reality that anchored, authored, and characterized him does the same for any one of us when we believe and trust the One who lives in our depths. Jesus came not so much to put some power or "thing" into us. Instead, he came to wake us up to this wonderful Gracious Mystery already living in our center. Our freedom to become who we are and to be able to make our Passover into God is greatly facilitated if we make this discovery and learn to live in fidelity to this inner Friend. But if our spiritual life is largely neglected or even impersonal and marked by a manner of religious formalism and legalism, then we miss making this discovery and risk significant danger to ourselves. We are then more vulnerable to the false gospel of consumerist fulfillment and the shallow philosophies of exaggerated individualism and the self-made person. We will lack sufficient spiritual depth to grow from experiences of our own limitations and failures, as well as the eventual encounters with our own aging, loss of physical freedoms, and dying process.

This inner authority or divinely given *exousia* is offered to each human being for the taking. When we trust and "access" it, our words and actions are transformed with new value and power. Thanks to our faith, hope, and love, we let God make our actions expressive of something good with divine power and eternal value. We create with God creating; we redeem with God redeeming. Our work and building up the kingdom or reign of God become an expression of God now at work and building. This is very much a part of our call. And when we understand this and accept it as our truth, then there is great meaning to our life; it opens us to much joy and blesses us with hope for ourselves, for others, and for the future of the world.

How do we come to know Jesus and the One he reveals, Abba Father? Certainly there are the obvious ways of catechetical instruction and reading, also moments of worship, faith-sharing, and retreats. But Christians have found that these means can leave one largely knowing about Jesus and God but still not knowing them personally, as the gospels invite us to do.

Knowing Jesus Personally

Experience and the wisdom of the many great men and women teachers of Christian prayer have stressed the primacy of regular, personal prayer focused upon the Jesus of the gospels as the best way for coming to know and love Jesus, as well as the One he reveals. To know Jesus well we must spend time with him in various stories of the gospels. There are many fruitful ways of doing this. The way of St. Ignatius and his Spiritual Exercises has us enter into one of these stories, with our imagination and the leading of his Spirit, place ourselves in the scene or identify with a character in it other than Jesus, and interact spontaneously. We might say words of praise, thanksgiving, sorrow, love, hope, or ask for healing. We can be drawn to respond with love and reverence as we see fit in the story. In engaging in this intimate kind of prayer we are not going back two thousand years, as if we are pretending we were a contemporary of Jesus. Rather, thanks to our faith in the risen Jesus who lives now and is available to us in every present moment, we engage the Jesus of the present moment, even if we are doing so through one of the gospel stories of his birth, of feeding the crowds, of healing someone blind, or of being crucified. This is an encounter with the living Christ Jesus himself rather than with just an image or memory of him. Anytime we come with faith to a story of Christ, something of the spiritual effects of Jesus's actions described in the story takes place in our depths. In our depths something of God becoming human happens. Something of Jesus's healing, teaching, and calling us occurs. Something of his dying and rising for us takes place in us. The entire story of salvation and each of its chapters can unfold inside our being if we engage in this kind of patient, reverent, intimate prayer. What unfolds is a personal, intimate story of his doing what he does *for us*.

Ignatius stresses this personal dimension to be taken from each story we would contemplate and declares what becomes so powerful for us: that in our depths he becomes human for us *now*.[3] In terms of the spiritual realm where the divine Spirit can impact human spirit, there is no advantage of a believing contemporary of Jesus over any one of us praying now with faith and love on the scene. The same opportunity of grace and blessing is available to anyone having faith and a childlike openness to receive whatever the Spirit of God gives. Neither the century we live in nor the part of the world we live in is an obstacle to this Mystery of Christ unfolding in us and transforming our selves.

Knowing That Truly Enlightens

Ignatius encourages us to do this kind of prayer not just one time (at most one hour but it can be less) but three, four, or perhaps even five distinct times. This may involve five periods of prayer during one day of a retreat or five periods spread over five or more days.[4] Ignatius tells us explicitly to "ask for interior knowledge of the Lord, who for me has become man, that I may more love and follow Him." In more contemporary language this petition reads, "I ask for the grace to know Jesus intimately, to be able to love Him more intensely, and so to follow Him more closely."[5] In each successive period we are to return to whatever details of the scene drew our interest earlier and touched us. Here our spirit "tastes and savors" whatever has been drawing us deeper, to what is progressively simpler, deeper, quieter, more loving and beautiful. In this rich silence God's Spirit can communicate what is sacred and oftentimes beyond words, speaking in our depths what is divine and most profound. Regardless of how deep and still we can be when entering a gospel scene, God's Spirit will give us a new and deeper felt knowledge of Jesus as well as a deeper sense of our own selves as beautiful and precious to God.

Ignatius of Loyola describes something of the deepest and most intimate levels of this new knowledge that we might come to share in when he speaks about "the interior senses of the soul."[6] These are intuitive-like sensitivities of our soul that correspond to the five senses of our body. These capacities are activated by the Spirit of Jesus praying in us while we spend four or five distinct periods of prayer focusing on some aspect of a gospel scene. Ignatius gives a cursory sense of this progression through the story of Jesus's birth.[7] In each successive time God's Spirit draws our spirit to greater and greater detail, eventually to some aspect of this universally loved story so that through the Spirit praying in us we are opened up with childlike wonder to self-forgetting love for Jesus and a deep personal knowledge of him.

An Example

This might begin with our entering an animal shelter or cave and walking past some goats, sheep, and cattle asleep in the hay. It is a cold, damp night lit by an almost full moon in a clear sky, studded with stars. You discover a young couple in the back part of the shelter as they sit there in generous amounts of straw and hay and gather some warmth from a nearby fire. They sit on opposite sides of an animal's feedbox or manger while attending to their swaddled child lying in it. You come upon them in the quiet and introduce yourself. Then they to you. The three of you take some time to get to know each other a little and share in the wonder and love these new parents have for their baby. They ask you what brought you here, what you seek and hope for. After you speak to their questions, you ask the same of them. You take the time both to listen well to what they say of themselves and to what you said about yourself. You sense something of the guidance of God's Spirit going on in their lives as well as in your own.

Eventually your attention is drawn to one detail of this charming, tender story. Like the zoom lens of a TV camera moving gradually from a wide-angle picture to a close and narrowly framed view, your heart responds to the pull or lead of God's Spirit in you. This Spirit takes you to what corresponds most to your own disposition at that moment and to your own longings for love, assurance, and hope. Perhaps the Spirit prompts you to ask the parents to let you hold the child and they gladly consent, or maybe they offer this before you even think to ask. You do this, taking the infant and spending as long as you like simply holding him. Maybe there are words of love coming from you, relating to this infant Savior as an infant and at other times as an adult, maybe as teacher or healer, as the crucified One or risen Lord.[8] You are guided so sensitively, so delicately in the secret recesses of your soul to what for you at this time is the most attractive or engaging part of the Christ mystery. Most likely you will eventually be moved to cease all speaking, to simply rest and just be lovingly attentive to whatever aspect of this mystery of love you are drawn to enjoy. To say anything at this time might feel inappropriate, since to be in this state of soul often evokes silent awe and will move you to engage simply in a long, loving gaze at the Holy. As you hold this precious mystery of God, you might sense how you in turn are held by God as precious. A certain timelessness prevails in this profound stillness, since you will have, in spirit, "stepped into eternity," leaving for a while the world of time and space. You become lovingly present with all you are to this Gracious Mystery of Love, forgetting yourself, as your spirit "touches" Divine Spirit, while each of you rests in the other and the two become one.[9]

There is an amazing new knowledge of Jesus we grow into over time as we pray with our imagination on his life. As we learn to be increasingly still and silent yet alert, attentive, and open during the later periods of this kind of prayer, we are given a progressively deepening felt knowledge of Christ, of Abba, and of their graciousness. One or more of the interior senses of our soul awakens in us. A whole new kind of knowing begins to happen, a loving knowledge that those too self-protected, busy, or self-centered could never know. Who Jesus the Christ is and the One he calls Abba can in this kind of prayer touch the depths of our soul with a profound sweetness and joy; we can be granted some unmistakable intimations of divine beauty and love. Our soul might be bathed in love and overflow with a sense of humble unworthiness. Deep gratitude and praise will follow. We will have been blessed with a taste of heaven. We will have come to know a little of what Divinity is, something of who the Christ is, of who God is, maybe something of the glory in which Mary, the Mother of God, or any one of the other saints lives and moves.

St. Augustine of the fourth century spoke of "the eye of the heart" opening and "seeing" such realities as we learn to be still and contemplate.[10] Ignatius of Loyola points to the same kind of opening of the soul when he describes this spiritual event as a new seeing or hearing, or as a "smelling and tasting the infinite fragrance and sweetness of the Divinity, or of the soul and virtues of a person," perhaps that of Mary or Joseph or a shepherd.[11] He says that with one or more of these interior senses of the soul we might "touch, embrace, and kiss the places where such persons put their feet and sit," so moved are we by love and the deep desire to praise and love in return for divine love so abundantly poured out on us.

What a profound, intimate knowing this kind of encounter can be! How alive and immediate Jesus becomes for us. There is a new knowing, and it changes many of our values and priorities as it did for St. Paul. Fed with this sweet, heavenly manna, we can relate well to what he says: "Whatever gains I had, these I have come to consider a loss because of Christ. More than that, I even consider everything as a loss because of the supreme good of knowing Christ Jesus my Lord. For his sake I have accepted the loss of all things and I consider them so much rubbish [in some translations the word is 'dung'], that I may gain Christ and be found in him" (Phil 3:7-9).

Empowered to Love

To set us on the path of our Passover journey we are placed, then, with Christ in his great work of helping to bring forth the kingdom. Blessed with this new and intimate knowledge of him, we might very well be moved to give our life and every moment of it to a way of life that shares everything with Jesus: work and friendship, joys and sorrows, life, death, and confidence in the afterlife. We have been placed in a school of discipleship where we are to learn his way of living and letting God reign. We are not expecting some "messiah" to liberate us from economic or political demands and threats while establishing our own nation or world as superior to others. Rather, we begin to learn the way of Jesus to be much simpler and humbler, yet costing everything. It is to follow along the pathway of Jesus, a way of mercy and forgiveness, a way of radical trust and complete self-donation. This is the tried-and-true way into our destiny in God, to be completely given and poured out (Phil 2:5-11). It is the way the three Persons of the Godhead relate in the Godhead and the way God relates to each of us, while doing the unthinkable and the unexpected for us in Jesus. As we grow in the habit of meeting Jesus in our prayer, as described above, the traits of his Heart more and more appear in our own heart and its desires. The sketch of his face and eyes gradually takes shape in our depths,[12] thanks to the delicate, creative work of the Spirit, the Divine Artist. We are becoming in Christ a new creation. It is, however, anything but an uncontested process, as we are soon to see.

Questions for Discussion and Faith-Sharing

1. How would you describe your own sense of being mis-sioned? What does your mission involve? Was there any "River Jordan moment" that awakened you to this sense?

2. Under what circumstances do you get tempted to doubt God's affirmation of you as his beloved daughter or son? How do you handle such experiences?

3. What reconnects you to your inner "authority" or *exousia* and to God and God's empowerment? Describe what that is like for you.

4. Have you prayed before with the help of your imagination, as exemplified in this chapter? Can you describe any image or images given to you in prayer that had a significant impact on the way you look at God, yourself, and your mission?

Chapter Five

OBSTACLES AND HELPS ON THE JOURNEY

When we look at Jesus's life, his infancy and especially his public ministry, we observe in addition to the great interest of the crowds notable resistance as well, to him and to what he proclaimed. We witness powers deeply entrenched and quite invested in maintaining certain political, economic, and religious structures. These powers kept so many of the people feeling distant from and unacceptable to God. The religion of that time offered little or no hope to the majority. In Jesus, however, these people began to feel hope in God's love for them. Because of his great impact on these poor ones, Jesus was perceived as a threat to the power and careers of the religious leaders. He was feared by many of them, resented, even condemned and eventually eliminated in the name of a distorted version of Judaism.

When reading these gospel accounts we can be smug about their outcome and self-righteously point an accusing finger at those who resisted and killed Jesus. In doing so we can remain blind to the same dynamics of resistance in our own selves. We might think ourselves above such evil. Yet, Jesus, and St. Paul too, challenge us to know ourselves, really, and to recognize that our hearts are divided, marked by grace and sin, by light and darkness, and therefore needing, more than we even want to admit, the saving love of God to transform our hearts.

St. Ignatius of Loyola has us look at this sobering truth in his meditation titled "The Two Standards." It depicts a great battle, even an ongoing war between two armies, one led by Christ, the other by Satan. Ignatius envisions Christ calling us to join him in this battle, to labor with him in overcoming all the evils that beset the human family. This call will particularly confront anything in ourselves that is not in harmony with him. These obstacles Ignatius calls our "own sensuality and carnal and worldly love."[1] He describes Satan also calling us, attempting to seduce us and, when necessary, coercing us to be a disciple of his and join in his campaign to enslave people through fear, sensuality, greed, and other evils.

It is strange to speak about our having two vocations, one from Christ and one from Satan. Yet it is true. There are two opposing value systems we subscribe to, two very different ways to live and relate to each other: one is the kingdom of Christ (God) and the other the kingdom of Satan. In the meditation on the Two Standards Ignatius has us pray to know well the strategy of Satan's way as well as that of Christ's way. Such knowledge is essential to our living our call in Christ and contributing to the building of the kingdom. In other words, we need an appreciable, practical knowledge of these two ways to recognize and judge accurately in our daily experiences what influences or inspirations are coming from Christ's Spirit and which ones are coming from the Evil One.

A Strategy Seeking Our Downfall

The first step in the Evil One's strategy is to lure us to a consumerist lifestyle, or simply a disordered desire for material riches;

money and possessions would be an important goal of our life and career choices. We may not attain these goals, but what matters is simply persuading us to focus our hearts on them. The attraction is to security, self-reliance, and a sense of well-being one assumes would come with it.

The second piece of this strategy is a seductive appeal to our desires for recognition, honors, and superiority. We think that if we are going to be happy we need to attain a certain status, reputation, and acceptance among our peers and maybe even by a wider public. We like titles and rank, prestige and public recognition because they make us feel valued and important. Establishing our identities on something as shallow and fleeting as this can easily lead to our developing discriminatory and exclusionary attitudes toward some groups or individuals: race and ethnic groups, certain religions and denominations of one's own religion, specific nationalities, people of the opposite gender, and so on. It will harden our hearts toward the poor and make us judgmental toward those who disagree with us and whom we look upon as failures and sinners. But there comes a day when we will experience a certain emptiness and loneliness from embracing these values. In time these honors and applause will feel hollow and maybe even mock us for our having been so foolish to trust in them.

The third and final piece of this anti-kingdom strategy is blinding pride. This ploy seeks to get us to succumb to our desires for power and control. It can make us live and choose as if we were the center of the universe, or of whatever part of the world where we would want to be the center—such as in one's marriage or family, in a church committee, in the workplace with its hopes for advancement, or even in some place like our children's world of Little League baseball. This is an especially dangerous temptation when others defer to us, flatter us and, wittingly or unwittingly, encourage us to live out of our self-centeredness. We become our own god and lose sensitivity to our need for God.

There is a deliberate progression, then, in this strategy: riches ("this is mine") to honors ("look at me") to pride ("I AM"). By these three steps the Evil One "entices people to all other vices."[2] Again, we do not have to succeed in this quest for riches, honors, and pride. We simply have to try to live according to such values in order to be shaped by and ensnared in their stranglehold. This can happen in so many diverse ways: aggressively pursuing a career or living out of a false sense of humility and hiding our talents. It can happen in our being focused on clothes, personal appearance, and our public image. We can also succumb to such idolatry by habitually resenting and blaming others in our family or work setting in order to justify and build up our own hurting ego.

The Counter-Strategy

In his words and actions Jesus shows another way to those who would aspire to be his disciples. It is a counter-strategy that answers point by point the three steps of Satan's strategy.

Where Satan enslaves and coerces, Jesus the Christ "gently but insistently invites followers of all kinds and sends them forth to spread His Good News to all peoples, no matter what their state or condition." Where Satan entices us to desire and trust in material wealth for our security, Jesus invites us in the first step of his threefold strategy to "the highest spiritual poverty," and to desire, if God would be better served, that he would choose us to live our life in "actual [physical] poverty."[3] Jesus invites us to a relationship with himself and Abba and to trust that relationship and God's guidance and strength to be our security. "Highest spiritual poverty," then, implies deep trust of and loving dependence on God to be there for us in all circumstances. In living such an exalted spiritual value we leave it to God to provide in whatever circumstances he calls us to serve him. We would choose to trust the promise of God's Holy Spirit instead of indulging anxiety and a disordered seeking of security through our possessions. It is a call, then, to resist temptations to self-doubt, self-pity, and discouragement. We would reaffirm in faith, deeper than these negative thoughts and feelings, the invaluable gift of relationship (I am part of a "we"). This gift grounds us and gives us an identity more precious than gold. From this sacred point in our depths we would experience what Jesus experienced with the Spirit of his Father: namely, his authority (*exousia*) and power (*dunamis*) to stand firm in his love for us and do through him what he would do. These are great blessings in spiritual freedom, developments that usually take some appreciable time to grow into, but entirely possible when we continue to ask for such.

Then for step two of his strategy Christ invites us, over against the honors, flattery, and empty rewards of a self-serving world, to accept and live with the "contumely [rude, haughty language] and contempt"[4] of others. The Scriptures and St. Ignatius say that this kind of opposition sometimes accompanies those who try to follow Christ and imitate him. Christ invites us, then, to a freedom from being ruled by feelings of insecurity and habits of compulsive perfectionism and trying to make ourselves secure or prove ourselves superior to others. Our security and freedom, rather, would be grounded in Christ whom we have come to love and trust and want to imitate. We might be hurt but not deterred or paralyzed by criticism and negative judgments when we are dismissed for what we value and who we are trying to be in Christ. In fact, in some instances we might well experience the consolation of communion with Jesus. We would know we are sharing with him something he underwent for us. We could accept our own limits and welcome constructive criticism, not being afraid to risk failure nor be threatened by the achievement of others, and not getting involved with others who promote relationships that are exclusive or discriminatory. Rather, freed from fear and jealousy, we would be blessed with an inclusive heart and an attitude of forgiveness that reaches out to stranger and even enemy.[5] A lofty state of spirituality here, yes, but clearly possible for those who truly want to live for Christ and give to him their whole selves.

In his third and final step, Christ invites us to humility, a radical truthfulness about ourselves as opposed to pride and arrogance that characterize the third part of Satan's strategy. We would experience ourselves as loved in Christ to such a degree that we would no longer have to or want to live a distorted, rugged individualistic spirituality. We would not be so proud nor be subject to feeling so unworthy that we could not ask for help; no longer would we have to win all the time or be the best in everything competitive. To have some authority or leadership role would give us the opportunity to serve in enhancing the freedom and progress of others, rather than using it to gain special favors or honors for ourselves. Feeling discouraged would not overwhelm us as it might have done so before. Instead, we would have gained a certain inner equanimity to be able to trust God's promise at a level deeper than the feelings of discouragement. Being in touch with our own truth would help us be rooted in gratitude, more accepting of others as they are, more ready to forgive, more patient and nonjudgmental.[6]

Humble people know that life is a gift, that each moment and every encounter is a gift waiting to be discovered. The root of all sin, in Ignatius's judgment, is ingratitude, ignorance, and forgetting one's blessings. Persons caught in pride and self-centered thinking are not free enough to look at life this way; it makes little sense to them. Humble persons who have genuinely accepted God's merciful, unconditional love in their own lives are free to be with people different than they are, different even in political and religious values or beliefs. They can still be gracious, respectful, and Christlike. They can trust the Spirit of God at work in these others and not identify them with their differences.

If we come to be so blessed to love Christ as the greatest love of our life, we will desire to serve as he did, without reward, and to suffer as he did, without retaliation. This great love for him will lead us to unite our experiences with his, consoled by this special knowledge of him and in our participation in his work to fill up "what is lacking in the afflictions of Christ on behalf of . . . the church" (Col 1:24).

It is through these three steps, then, that Ignatius says Christ will lead us to all the other virtues. What a profound empowerment this reflects; what an amazing enrichment and transformation this makes possible. More and more I will be living, no longer I, but Christ in me (see Gal 2:20).

The meditation on the Two Standards leads us, then, to make a fundamental choice regarding how we are going to live our lives: either we pursue what is essentially an ego-centered self trying to be in control and assure our security; or, we open up to the invitation of Christ and seek to be mentored and practiced in his school of wisdom and love. To accept Christ's invitation is to live out of the humble truth of ourselves, while accepting the claims of God and people on our time, resources, and energies. We would be letting go of many of our plans and trusting in a much greater plan: God's loving and meaning-filled plan in and for our life. The Ten Commandments guide us to right action, while the eight Beatitudes, special wisdom sayings of Jesus, instruct us in how to be, how to imitate Jesus. These values are showing mercy; expressing gentleness in manner; being a peacemaker; being single focused in seeking God in all things; hungering and thirsting for what is just and then being willing to suffer for it; mourning the spiritual shortcomings of the world, including one's own, while trusting in Christ's promise to redeem us from this condition; and finally, the foundation of all the virtues, being poor in spirit. To be poor in spirit is to recognize our own human limitations, powerlessness, and need for God while allowing God to be God in our lives. These sayings, then, name eight principal ways for living out the strategy of Christ. They give us a glimpse of what we as individuals and as a world communion in Christ will become someday.

The Importance of Ongoing Discernment

To choose to accept Christ's invitation requires more than sincerity and good intentions on our part. It demands our learning to discern, that is, to recognize what experiences are tending to bring us closer to God, toward a felt increase of faith, hope, and love; and which ones are tending to lead us away from God, a felt decrease in faith, hope, and love. It is after discerning that we make the choice either to go with the tendency, the direction of the movement, or to resist it. Discernment is for people who want to live their spiritual journey in God, with the habit of faith-consciousness. They will want to make choices informed by the knowledge of the ways of Christ and Satan, and so they learn what it means to be consoled by God and how, through deception, the Evil One can console us, only to betray us later. They learn the typical ways in which desolation can strike us and why it might come upon us; they especially learn the practical ways Ignatius offers us through his discernment principles for resisting desolation and actively countering the influence of the Evil One.

All Jesuits, that is, members of the Society of Jesus, are mandated by St. Ignatius to do a daily examen or review of the consolations and desolations of their day, to focus on the primary movement of their soul on that day, and pray in gratitude for the blessings of the day, especially if the primary movement was consoling. If the primary movement has been one of desolation and the person has succumbed to that movement (e.g., anger, fear, envy, unkind thoughts or words), then it is a moment for apologizing to God, asking for forgiveness, and promising to do the same to anyone who might have been hurt by the actions that followed from the desolation. If the movement was of desolation but the person did not succumb, then there may be special blessings and growth that happened because of the struggle. Again, much reason for thanking God for these gifts.

Many other Christians use the same method for themselves because they find it so practical. It gives them through practice greater and greater confidence in being able to understand the "language" and initiatives or communications of God's Holy Spirit. They gain an active knowledge of how to cooperate with God's Spirit in protecting themselves from the harm the Evil One intends.

Methods for Discerning God's Will

Besides a daily exercise of discernment in reviewing one's day, followers of Christ find it necessary at times to make important decisions that significantly affect their life in Christ and their relationships with God, neighbor, and self. Discerning God's will in our life is a central piece of Ignatius's spirituality. He and the original Jesuits practiced discernment when needing to make plans for the ministries they would commit themselves to worldwide. Whether they were discerning God's will with regard to choosing a particular mission or when considering the specifics of an already chosen mission, they used one or more of three methods.

The first is the rather rare case of being surprised with God's enlightenment. Whether experienced in a dramatic or quiet way, we are drawn in our will so that there is no way we can doubt what God is calling us to do. An example from the Bible is Saul getting knocked to the ground while on his way to persecute followers of Jesus and then awakening to Jesus's call for him to proclaim to Jews and Gentiles Jesus as Lord and Savior. Another example is of Levi, the hated tax collector; in the midst of collecting taxes, he is called, unexpectedly, to be a follower of Jesus.

We use the second method when we are experiencing numerous feelings, that is, consolations and desolations about two or more options for choice. It is these feelings we pray about and we use Ignatius's discernment principles in guiding our recognition of which feelings are leading us to the best of the possible choices, which option will bring us closer to God and bring forth God's greater glory in us and others.

The last method is used when we are not being significantly moved in our feelings with consolations and desolations. We then resort to a thinking process. We state clearly the options in front of us, gather all the needed data relevant to each option, and then list all possible reasons for and against each option for choice. We pray over these reasons, again using Ignatius's discernment principles to help us recognize the option that will realize God's greater glory in ourselves and in others. That greater glory will be manifest in terms of the realization of God's saving work and transformation of human beings in Christ. It will be seen in the progress persons make in knowledge and love of God, of neighbor, and of themselves.

The Prerequisite for a Trustworthy Discernment of God's Will

In each of these methods for decision making, the most important step is our opening to God's Holy Spirit, to wanting what God wants in this situation, and especially to being sufficiently free in spirit from any attachments in feelings and thoughts about the options that might compete with God and his will. Experience shows that most of the work of doing a discernment of God's will is done precisely in this area of becoming sufficiently free and open to allowing God to lead the process and discover what option will be best for God, for ourselves, and for those who will be served by the choice.

Ignatius has a meditation titled Three Pairs of Men[7] that engages this issue; it complements the meditation on the Two Standards in that the Two Standards seeks true knowledge of Christ's way and the way of Satan. In this meditation the person who prays seeks the freedom to love Christ more than any option or outcome and so be free enough to choose the option that would be the most conducive to Christ being loved and served. In short, to know the way of Christ is not enough to assure that we will choose it. Being free to choose the option that is God's will and fosters Christ's greater glory is a further gift in a discernment process. It is a blessing to be saved from being blinded or weighed down by our attachments, by the Evil One's strategies. We are made free to choose what is more in keeping with the values of the kingdom of Christ. Ignatius's focus in all these methods, then, is for us to be moved to this freedom by a growing love for Christ. These great gifts of love and freedom are given during prayer focused on Christ. Over time we come to know and love him as the great treasure and eventually as the greatest love of our life. We come to love him more than any option. He is the "inner star" or compass guiding us. Whatever we would choose, then, would flow from our love for him and deep desire to honor and serve him and deepen our friendship with him.

The Gift of the Paraclete

Once we take seriously the call of Christ, we soon discover the marvelous gift of the Holy Spirit, the Paraclete. Perhaps this discovery comes most in our practicing discernment and feeling the need for enlightenment and empowerment to act on what we discern to be Christ's call. Experiencing our insufficiency and sometimes powerlessness to live the demands of this new life sharpens our sense of how real and how close is this inner divine friend and guide.

In St. John's gospel Jesus speaks of the Paraclete as a Comforter (John 15:26; 16:7) and as the "Spirit of truth" (John 15:26; 16:13). Sometimes the word is translated as Helper or Advocate, as in a judicial setting to mean a lawyer or counsel for the defense.[8] Jesus emphasized that the Spirit would testify or witness to him as authentic and guide us to the fullness of the truth. The Spirit would also reprove the world opposed to God's kingdom for its sin of unbelief (John 15:26; 16:8, 13). Followers of Jesus experience this Gift usually as inner Guide who enlightens, showing us what is true; as Enabler who strengthens us to do the truth with love; finally, as deepest Friend who brings us into union with God, with neighbor, and especially with our true selves. To say this differently, we are re-created in Christ: our knowing is transformed, our loving is transformed, and we ourselves are transformed. All the best of our God-given potential unfolds and is brought into an integrated whole; our "house" is more and more made fit for the Father, Son, and Spirit to make their home in us (John 14:23).

In this re-creation the Spirit blesses us with three virtues, that is, habits and strengths of the soul that are the foundation of the entire spiritual life. They are faith in God and God's love for us; hope in God's promises in Jesus, strengthening us to trust God to provide for and give us the courage to risk for God; finally, charity, the greatest of the virtues, to empower us to love more and more selflessly. Charity transforms every other virtue while informing, unifying, and directing all aspects of our person toward God. It drives out fear and guilt, heals our shame, and empowers us to act with the mind and Heart of Christ. Our charity will be proportionate to the degree of maturity of our faith and hope.

Gifts and Fruits of the Holy Spirit

While we might compare these three foundational virtues to the flooring, walls, windows, and roofing of a house, along with its heating, electrical, and water facilities, so we might compare the gifts and fruits of the Holy Spirit to all that complete and beautify the interior of the house, making it truly a home fit both for God and for ourselves.

The fruits of the Spirit-Paraclete are the first indications of our transformation in Christ. They are described by St. Paul in his letter to the Galatians as follows: love, joy, peace, patience, kindness, generosity, faithfulness, gentleness, and self-control. "They are nine aspects of the mind of Christ, dispositions of Jesus . . . proving that [he] is living in us."[9] There are certainly more of the Paraclete's blessings than these, but Paul implies this when citing something of the variety of God's innumerable blessings. The impact of the Paraclete is diverse and extensive when empowering us to live with the virtues of faith, hope, and charity.

The gifts of the Holy Spirit are considered more mature or advanced blessings of the Spirit-Paraclete.[10] The first four pertain to the transformation in Christ of our mind or intellect, namely, whenever we seek to know something, understand, make judgments, and/or discern. They are knowledge, understanding, counsel or discernment, and finally wisdom. The last three gifts pertain to the transformation of our will through which we love and make decisions and choices. They are fortitude, piety (or perseverance), and fear (reverence) of the Lord.[11]

The gift that bridges both groups of gifts is wisdom; it integrates our knowing and willing, the two activities that most clearly image our likeness to God. Wisdom is a "certain kind of seeing and knowing which are permeated with the perception of God himself. This seeing and knowing arise intuitively [within us]."[12] It is a knowing that is the fruit of a shared life with God. We come to see as God sees, feel about things the way God feels about them, even our sufferings and failures, because we have, so to speak, taken on the mind and Heart of God. In God's wisdom we can "see" a truth, even when we are troubled at the surface of daily happenings. Deep down, then, we have come to the peace only God can give. We know intuitively that we are known, loved, and welcomed by Gracious Mystery just the way we are in every detail. This is all "the result of direct communion with God . . . experienc[ing] in love that which most uniquely constitutes God as God."[13] We are able to relish, savor, and delight in God as well as in the beauty of God's creation. It gives us a taste for only God and whatever is in God and of God. All other things and situations, whatever not related to God, feel empty, boring, and unpleasant, sometimes even bitter to our spirit. We instinctively shun the strategies of Satan and gravitate to the life and ways of Christ because we have grown through these gifts (and fruits) to know and love him as well as to will and love as he would.

The Gift of Jesus

While it is true that Jesus was first given to us at Nazareth, and then in his life, passion, death, and resurrection, there is a sense in which he is being given to us more fully during this time following Pentecost. Jesus made it very clear in his final hours that the Spirit-Paraclete would take what he said and reveal it more fully, completing his revelation (John 16:13-15). As time passes and the church ponders the Scriptures and the church's reflections on them for over two thousand years, we appreciate more and more the Father's gift of Jesus. God cannot speak anything deeper nor more intimate than Jesus. In him God gives us his Heart, his ultimate self-communication, that which is most precious to him. Jesus is God's Beloved in whom he is "well pleased" (Matt 3:17; 17:5).

Over time followers of Christ and his strategy come to treasure Jesus as the greatest discovery of their lives. In Ignatian spirituality Jesus is experienced as "gift for me" and in the "now," given not only to me but to all in the church and even to everyone in the world. When experiencing him, especially in his manner of dying, disciples are so often moved to a great love for him. Love never before experienced like this and being so personal moves disciples to offer themselves totally, in whatever way Christ might be best served in the work of the kingdom. He becomes one's deepest truth and first love. He opens up our soul like no one else.

A number of titles applied to Jesus in the Scriptures will come alive for us: for example, living water, Light of the World, Bread of Life, the resurrection and the life, the Vine, our Teacher and Master, prophet, Servant, Savior, Son of Man. We might come to know him personally through our being healed in body or maybe by being freed in soul, for example, from a dark past accompanied by fears, shame, and/or guilt. We might identify with certain persons in the gospels and experience his compassion, his mercy as they did: for example, the Samaritan woman at the well; the man born blind; the woman using her hair to wipe the feet of Jesus, wet because of her tears; or Peter being forgiven for his threefold denial of Jesus. All of these are compelling stories of being found by God's merciful love.

Jesus is the supreme gift of God to the world. He is given as our Way, Truth, and Life. He constitutes the original and primordial sacrament of God.[14] In him Divinity takes on humanity. In him God steps into time and space, enabling us to know and "touch" God. He is the icon[15] of God, *the* way for knowing God in the intimate, tender way Jesus's name for God implies, that is, Abba. He leads us to God and lets us experience his Abba as our own Abba, or Imma, Em, or Amma, if one prefers. What matters is our trusting and accepting God's gentle, never-ending welcome extended to us as a precious son or daughter, while allowing God to hold us next to his Heart. When we accept this divine gesture, we come to experience ourselves as known and loved for who we are. We also come to know and love Divine Love like no other way. It is especially in relating this way that we are transformed or divinized. Our whole being is ever seeking such an encounter, consciously and unconsciously, until we find it.[16]

The Gift of the Church

After the death, resurrection, and ascension of Jesus, the Spirit-Paraclete has continued to help us live our call by giving us the church, the community of believers, and its sacramental rituals. The church is so many things, but above all it is the sacramental continuation of Christ Jesus throughout history. As God's people, the church makes him present to each member of the church and to the whole world in all the ways he was present during his earthly life: in preaching, teaching, and healing. The church is not the kingdom of God, as some in the history of the church have tried to make it out to be. Rather, the church is in service of the kingdom. It is meant to prepare its members for the coming of this ultimate reality. While divine in origin, the church is at the same time made up of sinful people continually needing repentance, conversion, and healing. Born from the open side of the crucified Christ pierced by the Roman soldier's lance,[17] the church is sustained and animated by the Spirit-Paraclete as its soul. The water that flowed from the pierced Heart of Christ anticipated baptism, the spiritual birth of the church's members. The blood that flowed from his side anticipated the Eucharist, the spiritual nourishment we need for our Passover journey.

The other sacraments of the church celebrate Christ's ministering to his members in special moments of their life with God: for example, in their repenting and needing forgiveness; in being anointed when sick in body and/or spirit; in being strengthened and confirmed in their baptismal commitment with an anointing and its deeper outpouring of the Spirit-Paraclete; in the blessing of a man and woman marrying each other while they commit themselves to Christ and to each other to live as a sign of the love of Christ and the church for each other; finally, in ordaining certain members of the church to act as official representatives of the church in proclaiming the Gospel and in providing for the sacramental needs of its members.

In essence, the church is the people of God, a communion of men, women, and children who profess belief in Christ and have been baptized into the mystery of his dying and rising (Rom 6:3-14). It is the family of God's adopted sons and daughters. Some are still on pilgrimage to God, living this earthly life with hope; some have passed from this world but are in need of further purification and are not yet fully transformed in Christ; finally, there are those who have completed their journey home to God, fully transformed in Christ, and live forever as part of the communion of saints.

It is possible for those who are not water-baptized and/or do not identify with the Christian church to realize many of God's blessings. This is so because, with the aid of the Spirit of Christ offered to all, they know and love the Christ hidden in their neighbor and in their own selves. Anyone who over the years tries to live in fidelity to his or her conscience and the voice of love and goodness within knows and serves Christ. The fruits of the Spirit in one's life testify to this truth. The parable of the sheep and goats in Matthew's gospel, chapter 25, makes this quite clear. Still, there is an advantage to all who make this Passover journey to enjoy the many means of support and growth available in the community of Christ's brothers and sisters, with its Scriptures and sacraments.

It must be granted that the experience of church for some has been anything but Christian, but rather has wounded them and even been a source of scandal. Still it is true that where church is lived with integrity and love, there Christ will be found and participation in the church's life will build up its members far more than if they should try to make their Passover journey as individuals.

Church, preexisting its members, "makes them what they are by empowering them to move from 'death' to 'life' . . . The Christian community brings its members into being, the new being of authenticity."[18] It proclaims that all of life, even in its most seemingly ordinary moments, "carries" the Divine with it; every human experience, then, becomes a spiritual, religious experience when we respond to God in the moment with faith, hope, and love.

The Gift of the Bible

As church, the people of God are a people of the book, the Holy Scriptures. As followers of Jesus and his Way, the church finds its primary resource for knowing him in the four gospels. The gospels are not biographies but, rather, faith-inspired portraits of Jesus as the incarnation of the God of the Jewish covenant. They proclaim Jesus as the new Moses and bringer of salvation, of a new and everlasting covenant meant for everyone, Jew and Gentile.

The gospels did not preexist the church, as if they were blue-prints provided before the experience of church. Instead, they are a product of the early church's life. Through an oral and written tradition, this early "church maintained the memory of Jesus and his mission. . . . [It] selected and preserved those moments of Jesus's life that meant the most to a believer. The church etched its own rich experience onto the very contents of the gospel. . . . From the church came the evangelists, those creative men to whom we are indebted for the gospels."[19] With these four portraits of Jesus and the letters of Paul, Peter, Jude, and John, the Letter to the Hebrews, and the book of Revelation, as well as the holy books of the Jewish Scriptures, Christians encounter the Spirit-Paraclete revealing Jesus more and more and guiding us, even praying in us, as our deepest friend. This divine friend makes possible to any and all in the human race the way for our realizing our destiny in God to become authenti-cally human and divinized in Christ.

The Eucharist

The preeminent moment for the church is the time when we, its members, gather around the altar to celebrate the Lord's Supper. We celebrate the mysterious, wonderful transformation God is accomplishing in history, through Christ: first, in our own lives and in our communion as God's people; also in those who do not formally and consciously know Christ but are obedient to his Spirit-Paraclete; and even in those who do not know him, do not put any faith in him, and even oppose him. Passages of the Bible are read to remind us of the Passover journey we are all making to God and to encourage us to faith in God and hope for salvation in Christ Jesus. These readings especially renew our call to help bring forth God's justice, "an enduring attitude of loving tenderness that constantly affirms the dignity and sacredness of all . . . . a justice and peace . . . with its compelling vision of merciful concern for all." This is what it means "to 'pass-over' into God's 'land' of freedom and peace," to "commit ourselves as one community to live what we just heard."[20]

This communion with God and with each other is sealed in blood, the ultimate gift of life by none other than God become flesh in Jesus. It begins with an exchange of gifts between God and ourselves. We present and dedicate to God our lives as they are at that moment, symbolized by gifts of bread and wine offered up. These gifts in turn are taken by God and, through the power of the Holy Spirit, are so transformed that now they become a completely different reality whose essence is no longer bread and wine. Instead, they are now the Body and Blood of Christ sacramentally present. This mystery of faith is based on trusting the word of Jesus, as demonstrated in chapter 6 of John's gospel. As we give ourselves to God, like the boy with the five loaves and two fishes or the widow with the two coins, Jesus in turn gives himself to us in this awesome, unique way. Our humble gifts have become multiplied infinitely in the gift of Jesus given back. This we ratify, the covenant as well, whenever we eat his Body and especially when we drink his Blood.[21]

As church, then, we are to go forth on mission, back to our daily lives, with the power of the Word and empowering presence of Christ's Body and Blood accompanying us to be lights and salt to all we serve. As God's people we keep coming back time and again to celebrate this most important prayer until the power of this Mystery of Love takes hold in our hearts and transforms us into the compassion of Jesus in our own day. We become what we receive, then, the Body and Blood of Christ. The form or structure of this ritual is basically the same every time we pray the Eucharist. What is new each time is what is going on in our lives and in the world that day, different from what we offered the last time we participated in the Eucharist; this is what is lifted up with Christ's offering to the Father. What the Father gives back to us, then, are Christ, his Spirit, and the

Spirit's gifts tailored to our call to be other Christs in whatever ways we are to love and serve that day or in the days till our next Eucharist.

The Gift of the Saints

One of the most effective helps to those who aspire to follow Christ and to guard against the influence of anti-Christ values is the lives of the saints, men and women who lived their lives for Christ as outstanding examples of Christlike love and compassion. We love the particularities of their stories and visualizing the chapters of their journey to God. Their lives encourage our own dreams and hopes to live life deeply, authentically, lovingly, even heroically, and spur us to act on God's inspirations in us. Because these exemplary Christians now live in the resurrection as members of the communion of saints, we often seek their friendship and wisely ask them to intercede for us with God as we try to imitate them in living for Christ.

The Gift of Mary, Mother of God

There is, however, no saint that has been a source of strength and spiritual refuge for God's people as much as Mary, the mother of Jesus. The gospels of Luke and John as well as the first chapter of the Acts of the Apostles and parts of the book of Revelation witness to her preeminent place in the saving work of Jesus. There are numerous scenes in the New Testament that together form a collage of images of her divinely constituted role: from her "fiat" to the angel Gabriel and conceiving the Savior all the way to her being in the midst of the apostles and some women as she and they gather for prayer and wait for the coming of the Spirit-Paraclete and birth of what would be known as the church. Throughout the centuries so many of the church's faithful have found God's guidance, courage, discernment, and healing by praying to Mary. Numerous shrines honoring her can be found throughout the world, as well as many statues.

Countless people come to God through praying her rosary. Mary is not the focus of our prayer; rather, she is our preeminent friend and companion leading us to Jesus so that we might receive from him the fullness of life she has received.

The most intimate and maybe mystical of all the biblical scenes involving Mary comes when Jesus is dying, when he says to her, "Woman, behold, your son." And then to the Beloved Disciple standing next to the cross, "Behold, your mother." Saint John, the gospel writer, then adds, "And from that hour the disciple took her into his home" (John 19:26-27). The Beloved Disciple represents any one of us who believes in Jesus as the Savior, as the resurrection and the life . . . and has dared to let him kneel before us and accept his invitation to let him wash our feet and yes, even to rest our head on his Heart. Such can happen in the depths of prayer, and so we come to know a joy and strength beyond all expectation.

Once we accept this invitation, we can own for our own selves Jesus's final words in this scene: "Behold, your mother." These words issue a gentle challenge for us to discover how his mother is at the same time our own mother and to know through experience the various ways she is involved in birthing Jesus in us over and over again. When these words of Jesus come alive in us, we are then able to identify with the closing words: "And from that hour the disciple took her into his home." The phrase "into his home," in the original Greek, has a far richer meaning than what the words "house" or "home" usually mean. We could translate it, "he took Mary into his inner life, his inner being . . . into the depths of his being." There is, then, a major role God has given her in the life of each believer or "beloved disciple." It means "to introduce her into the dynamism of one's own entire existence."[22] She is described at the Second Vatican Council as "pre-eminent and as a wholly unique member of the church, and as its exemplar and outstanding model in faith and charity."[23]

Besides her extraordinary honor in being the one who brought the Savior to the world, it is this point about her being the type of the church that explains much of Mary's importance for us. All the favors shown to her are meant to anticipate the blessings God intends to work in each of us. God gives us Mary, conceived immaculately, conceiving virginally, free from sin, full of grace and, yes, raised up and assumed body and soul into heaven so that we will contemplate her as a type and model of what each of us and the church as one communion are to become on the Day of Christ. Christ is the firstborn of this new creation. Mary can be said to be the secondborn of a countless number of God's children destined to follow her and her Son into eternal life.

Numerous Other Helps

There are so many ways in which God gives us helps for living our call in Christ. I will end this chapter by mentioning a few of the more important ones.

One is the gift of friends, companions along the way. A true friend can support us in good times and bad, when we are wonderful and during those times when we are not so wonderful. In friendship God reveals himself in shared conversation, in shared laughter and shared beauty, in struggles to understand each other, in forgiving and reconciling, in accepting the other as other and as gift. Some refer to friendship as the eighth sacrament, so close can it bring us to God.

Also the gifts of family and community. We are made to belong, to be connected, to be welcomed, and to learn how to love. Sometimes our ethnic, cultural background opens up many gifts to us. Sometimes our national heritage and its political struggles bring us joy and meaning; sometimes we are challenged to speak out against something unjust and immoral.

Another is the gift of those who are poor, the stranger, the sick, those who are dependent and need our help. Caring for children or the elderly in family life can be two examples. Or meeting someone who lives with the barest of necessities, at the edge of economic survival. We might at first relate to these kinds of people as a distraction or interruption in our schedule, yet some of the richest encounters with Christ are waiting for us in such meetings. Situations of this kind draw us out of ourselves and mirror back something of our own vulnerability and powerlessness, what the Bible would term our poverty. They move us along in our Passover journey and in God's school of love to deeper awareness, selfless presence, and compassionate response.

Then there is the gift of our work, the expression of our time, talent, and efforts. Meaningful work can bring forth the best in our spirit, give us purpose, and offer us the opportunity to be creative, to invent, and feel competent in what we do and fulfilled when seeing the fruit of our efforts. Work is meant to be ministry. Good work done out of love for Christ and with him is cocreative, since it is united to what God is doing in history to bring forth his kingdom. When we bring this faith perspective to our day, even the most mundane and repetitious acts become kingdom-building acts. They are ministry to Christ and are part of what is joined to the offering of Christ to the Father during the Eucharist.

Leisure complements our work and is another important help to our spiritual development. The command of the Sabbath, to rest from our work and give thanks to God, is meant to dispose us for this critical piece of a wholesome life worthy of being called Christian. Hobbies and sports, time in nature, going to a movie, or taking a relaxing bath are examples of such moments. They can be special ways of encountering Christ and his gracious love for us.

The gift of the animal, plant, and mineral parts of creation are so much a part of God's blessings for our journey. The enjoyment of a pet, a walk in the woods, a swim in a lake, viewing a full moon or beautiful sky at sunset, working the soil to produce beautiful flowers and delicious vegetables or fruit can be so helpful in bringing balance to our life.

The arts are a special instance of how God helps us in making our Passover journey. They are essential to our spiritual health, bringing us to beauty that centers us, calms us, delights us. The nineteenth-century Russian novelist Dostoevsky, in his novel *The Idiot*, wrote that the world will be saved through beauty. This is so intuitively reassuring, most probably because the arts encourage the contemplative in us and bring us to experience what is simple and beautiful, what is emotionally moving while connecting us with Truth and Goodness itself. The arts are the one universal language in the world. They suggest endless holy possibilities for our soul and often hint at divine Beauty.

Last, there is the gift of the sciences. What God has given to the world, thanks to the curiosity and intelligence of human beings studying the nature of the atom, the seas, the earth and sky, including the cosmos, is simply breathtaking. How awesome the changes to our world because of the microscope, the telescope, the computer, and the internet. What we humans have developed through our application of the sciences to technology has revolutionized cultures and civilizations. The danger in many instances has been for us to take these gifts of God and make them into our modern domesticated gods, so fascinating can they be. But for those who do not forget the Creator and Giver of all these gifts, any one of them can have genuine sacramental value for us, move us to awe and gratitude, and hold us in wonder at who this one and only God is. We are also humbled with the realization that through our lives we are helping to bring to fulfillment the great mystery of the unfolding of Christ in all of creation.

Questions for Reflection and Faith-Sharing

1. Name the pieces of the anti-kingdom strategy you think significantly affect those in your national, ethnic, racial, or gender groups; family, or marriage.

2. Which piece(s) of Christ's strategy challenge(s) you the most? Explain why.

3. How do you experience the Spirit-Paraclete? As friend or artist or how?

4. Which of the fruits and gifts of the Spirit do you sense you need most at this time in your life?

5. In what ways do you experience the church being holy? Explain.

6. Do you experience God in your daily work? Do you "find" God in your marriage, in religious community, or in being single; in family; in the poor, the weak, the needy, and the sick; in leisure, the arts, the sciences, nature; in friends or enemies and those who make you suffer; in Mary, the mother of God, or any of the other saints? Name the ones in which you especially experience God present and active.

Chapter Six

LOSING CONTROL, BECOMING MORE FREE

There is only so much we can do in our efforts to make something of the helps God gives us. There come times when our efforts are largely futile or even get in the way of our spiritual growth. Experiences of personal failure and loss, a serious accident, being victimized, becoming seriously ill, or simply undergoing the aging process—events like these teach us we are not in control of our life. We have to learn to surrender and let God take the lead more than before (Exod 14:13-14). To be brought into this dimension of our journey to God is Good News but often feels like bad news. It brings us gifts that come in no other way. We have to die to a number of ways and habits in our thinking, speaking, and acting, in the ways we pray and image God, in the ways we understand God and our own selves. We have to be taken by God through some of these kinds of experiences to appreciate the ultimate powerlessness of humanity. Like the silkworm spinning its cocoon, dying there after a long wait and coming out as a gorgeous butterfly, we must go through what is an amazing metamorphosis to be born to the fullness of life in Christ.[1] To fight this process is to risk being spiritually stillborn or, at least, much less than what we could have become.

Jesus as the Way

To show us the way through this part of our journey into God, the Father gives us his Son.

Jesus fully embraces our human condition and shares in the more difficult parts of it: privation, loneliness, failure, hunger, being frustrated, hated, feared, and betrayed. He struggled terribly with his dying. Eventually he surrendered to his situation as something he knew in prayer to be his call and God's mysterious way. It is not that God intended Jesus to die the awful death he did die. Rather, God willed Jesus to be faithful to his call, *even if* it meant that he had to lay down his life in order to be faithful to his mission in the face of arrogant, violent people. Only in this sense did God will Jesus's death. It is clearly not what God wanted in the first place.

It was Jesus's total "yes" to God in this terrible situation that assures the salvation of the world (Rom 5:18-19). His "yes" is what gives eternal meaning to our own losing control and suffering. In trusting God and making this choice we give God permission to move in our lives and take us to places in the Spirit we would otherwise never be able to go. God guides us, then, to situations in our Passover journey that we simply do not understand but will later (John 21:18). This is the same paradoxical truth that was at the heart of Jesus's own sufferings. As our own journey unfolds and we encounter sufferings and powerlessness, we find the same basic meaning emerging for ourselves. God accomplishes in us aspects of our salvation that cannot be realized except through loss and giving God permission to act in us.

Letting Go, Letting God

Jesus is divine, but this truth is invoked too readily by many to make an exception in their minds for Jesus when it comes to his experiencing limitation, of not knowing certain things and needing to learn. Some cannot conceive of his needing to gain clarity and guidance through prayer, of having to wait on an outcome about which he did not have foreknowledge, of struggling and truly being afraid. Many Christians have been formed to emphasize Jesus's Divinity so much that they cannot take seriously his humanity, his being like us in all things but sin (Heb 4:15). For some, having not sinned makes Jesus less than human: that to be human means to be flawed and prone to mistakes. Human nature is identified with failed humanity rather than with what it can be in Christ.

The Christian Scriptures proclaim that all of what it means to be fully human is seen in Jesus. This includes suffering loss, pain, abandonment, and death. We want to flee all of this, deny it, maybe even compromise our souls to escape it. We would rather put Jesus on a pedestal and insist that somehow he is not affected by these humbling aspects of being human because he is divine. Jesus, however, fully human and fully divine, shows suffering and death to be part of our humanity and how to let God do something wonderful with it.

The stark truth is that Jesus fulfilled his mission more by what he allowed to be done to him than by what he did. More powerful than all of his spoken words when preaching, healing, and teaching was the unforgettable "Word" he "spoke" when he hung on the cross. In that pitiful state he had to *be* the Word, everything that previously, in the freedom of a young man, he was able to proclaim in speech.

There are days when we find ourselves in a similar situation. When we are healthy and productive, able to plan our day, make appointments, experience ourselves being successful, we then feel we have purpose and meaning. Yet the reality of Jesus challenges us to recognize that the greatest meaning of our life is offered us when we are dependent, when we have lost control. Experiences like "burnout," being seriously ill for a lengthy time, being paralyzed, or waiting and waiting for death while in a nursing home can be such examples. Other instances may include becoming disillusioned with our marriage or grieving the end of it; suffering the death of one of our children, especially a suicide; losing our job or home; feeling scandalized by and indifferent to the church in the face of her sinfulness; or having a full-blown faith crisis. These are moments of major collapse of our world as we knew it. We are thrown into an experience of feeling abandoned and unloved, of seeming nothingness. These trials cast us into the same state of being in which Jesus found himself in the last days of his life when he stood overlooking the city of Jerusalem and wept at what could have been, had he not been rejected by the leaders and many of the people. He had given his all during the last three years and he was misjudged, scorned, and rejected.

Still, God took this disaster and made it into what we call Good Friday. God does the same for us when, with trust, we give him room to do what only he can do in our human failures and sufferings. It is during such situations that God can do his most significant and transforming work in our depths. Jesus invites us, coaxes us boldly to trust in him and to present ourselves to God with courageous faith and patient surrender.[2] It is in these kinds of situations where God works the more dramatic instances of Easter in our lives.

The question is, Do we believe God can do this or not? Is Jesus that real for us? Does the story of his being raised up from death make that much of a *practical* difference to us and in the way we look at our losses when they take us beyond our control? Do we trust enough to choose deliberately to live in new ways that keep us open to such transforming love? I myself am challenged when trying to cope with family situations and the trials of other people I love during their struggles with complicated emotional and moral issues. My staying connected to them, keeping them steadily in prayer, while commending them to the saving providence of God is the only way I know of living with trust in Christ and waiting on God to do what only God can do.

Loved Like Never Before

Jesus has preceded us in this same mysterious journey that requires surrender and trust. When it is our turn to walk a frightful part of our journey, we can meet him in our darkness and experience his reassuring presence. He knows what we are going through since he himself has been there before and his Spirit is with us through it all. He has been through the worst of what any human being could go through. The gospels show us horrible things having been done to Jesus, yet God allowed this to happen to him so that no one could ever say to God, "You have no idea what I am going through!" In Jesus, God responds, "I have been there when you have felt most forlorn, most abandoned, most abused. I have been there, even though you have not felt my presence. I have been there for you. I know your pain. I have painfully allowed what was done to Jesus on Good Friday to be my way of being there with you and for you, when you felt most abandoned and, yes, crucified. In him, my Beloved Son, your brother and Savior, I have embraced you and shared in your pain. And I assure you this is not and will not be the last chapter of your story, just as it was not the last chapter of Jesus's story. Love is more powerful than death. Love has the last 'say'; if you trust me and my ways, it will have the last 'say' in this sad chapter of your life and in your whole life."

When we are going through our dark nights, our Gethsemane experiences, we need to heed the wise counsel of St. Teresa of Ávila (d. 1582). She says in the closing parts of her spiritual classic *The Interior Castle*, "Fix your eyes on the Crucified [One] and everything will become small for you."[3] Unless we fix the eye of our heart on him, the crucified and *risen* Savior, fear will hypnotize us and attitudes like resentment and hatred will squeeze the life of God out of our spirit. Dark moments like these can overpower our soul and we will more likely do things similar to what St. Peter the Apostle did during the trial of Jesus.[4] We will effectively deny Jesus and seek our security and meaning in something else.

The Dark Night

Saint John of the Cross offers insightful analysis of the origin of and divine purpose in the experiences of spiritual darkness. I know of no one as clear and profound as he is in helping us understand these difficult experiences of our Passover journey.

First, he speaks of experiences lived not by those whose lives are predominantly sinful but by people trying to live good lives yet are still unconverted in a number of ways. Some of their darkness comes simply from the human condition, some from the pain they and others bring upon themselves, often by the misuse of their God-given freedom. But sometimes it is God himself who provokes this darkness, out of love. Our first reaction is to think the "devil" is doing this, or that God has pulled away or even abandoned us.

It is possible that carelessness regarding our relationship with God has exposed us to spiritual danger, and the darkness that follows is letting us feel the consequences of our neglect. It is a wake-up call and a humbling. There are other times, however, when God is the protagonist. On such occasions God has not pulled away from us but, rather, has come closer to us, particularly to those parts in us still not in harmony with his Spirit and perhaps largely unconscious to us. In doing so God "pushes these disorders," so to speak, from the hidden, neglected "basement" of our being up into our everyday awareness, to the "first and second floors" of our "house." This can leave us feeling a certain emptiness and separation from God while wondering what we did to deserve such. It teaches us how un-Christlike we still are, in more ways than we would like to admit. But the initiative is with an all-loving God who cares enough to move us closer to a part of our truth, to make us really look at it, all for the sake of our greater purification and freedom in Christ.

John of the Cross calls this divine initiative "the inflow of God."[5] This inflow focuses not just on behaviors but more so on attitudes and values, that is, the roots of our behaviors. To explain God's transforming action John cites a central principle in his theology of the spiritual life, that "contraries cannot coexist."[6] We have to be freed from whatever is not Christlike in thought, memory, imagination, and will. Otherwise, any of these attitudes or values will be a "contrary," an obstacle to a deeper union with God. God moves closer in order to purge us of such spiritual contaminants that adulterate our relationship with him. Like a highly reputed surgeon, God heals us of what constitutes a certain spiritual sickness. We are taken to a place we would prefer not to go, to a place we could not reach on our own, even if we so desired. The help of a competent, spiritually sensitive psychotherapist and/or trained spiritual guide can many times prepare us to get at these core issues. Experience shows, however, that the needed purification and healing are a work that in the end God alone can bring about. All we can do is give our consent and cooperate with the process, to surrender and wait on God in courageous faith and hope.

Like the watchman waiting for the dawn (Ps 130:5-7), we are now more passive, actively passive, that is, than earlier when we made numerous efforts to change our behaviors. We are now far more led than leading. At a time like this we need to increase our prayer, adopt certain acts of penance, and make deliberate acts of self-abnegation. We will most likely be ready to "talk out" our soul, its feelings and movements, thoughts and disturbances, worries, temptations, and desires. It will seem this process becomes one great uprooting of what has been hidden from us till now. It is humbling and probably even embarrassing. We may discover, for example, that deep down we are very angry and wanting control, that over the years we have been unable to believe we are really loved by God, and so we are subject, for example, to resentments, self-pity, envious thoughts, and gossiping. When facing attitudes and behaviors like these, and at the same time gazing at him hanging there on the cross for us, we may weep at how meager our love and gratitude have been for him. How purifying, how purging and freeing such encounters can be. As we are exposed to the unforgettable love of Jesus, we are cleansed in heart and freed to choose to become more the people God has made us to be.[7] This entire process is the essence of purgatory, something of what it looks like in this life, as well as a hint of what it will be after our death. We will need God to finish his work of transforming us. Hopefully much or even most of it will be accomplished in this life.

It is this "inflow" of God, then, that causes the "dark night."[8] This night refers to a set of experiences God precipitates in us, not only to purify us but to greatly expand the capacities of our soul and wean us from earlier, less mature ways of encountering him. It can involve a "darkening" of the intellect or imagination, memory too, in that what used to be our way of praying with these usual ways of thinking, imagining, and remembering no longer bring us to God in the same way they did before. Now we are drawn to a simpler way of relating to God, of praying without concepts, images, and strong feelings. We are led to know God much more by a deep faith and trust than through our senses.

The way of faith and trust is absolutely necessary for knowing God as God is and for the completion of our Passover journey. To rely upon our own felt experiences of God/Jesus, fond religious memories and consoling images as our primary way for relating to God limits greatly our knowing God as God is, and of knowing ourselves as we really are in God's eyes. To grow into spiritual adulthood we have to step out in faith and cross over a bridge to God's side of the relationship, while surrendering our desire to know him through our own feelings and thoughts.[9] This is particularly true in the case of those invited by God's Spirit to a simpler way of prayer and more intuitive way of knowing, to what is classically called acquired contemplation. We become less and less able to pray fruitfully in a discursive way and with images. Instead, we are inclined to the prayer of "resting in the Spirit," to the prayer of being, of simply enjoying the presence of God while remaining attentively, lovingly silent. Faith in what God reveals in Jesus and trusting God's promise become enough for us. We have learned to walk by faith and not so much by sight, in the way we pray as well as in the way we live our day.

It can seem somewhat precarious to take up this invitation to live more by faith and leave behind familiar ways of praying and being with people. For many it feels like we have lost our way and that God has disappeared. It is as if God has hidden behind some cloud. In reality, as was said earlier, God has come closer to us. Our first instinct is to try to experience God in the former, more familiar ways. Our efforts can be likened to our attempting to focus our eyes on the palm of our hand while it is pressed against our nose. This is impossible! As time passes, though, we ease into a new way of praying, a way of more just being with God and trusting. God's self-communication is not as detectable as before. In many ways it is not detectable at all by our senses, except weeks or months later someone might notice a deeper peace in us and some other Christlike changes.

John of the Cross likens this new and more intense experience of God to the sun overpowering our eyes.[10] While our eyes will be flooded, even overwhelmed by the sun—if we are foolish enough to stare at it—we will see not light but total blackness. Likewise, God has come closer to our mind and heart, and our usual ways of thinking, imagining, and feeling are overwhelmed, "darkened," so to speak. They are simply incapable of receiving God in this new, more direct or immediate way God is giving himself to us. We learn to trust God leading us in all of this. We no longer fear that we have lost our way.

Storms and Trials

Deliverance from the previously mentioned spiritual obstacles present under the Standard of Satan and movement toward the glorious freedom Christ offers us can leave us battle-weary. John of the Cross speaks specifically of "storms and trials" in our five senses and deeper in our spirit where we remember, think, and make choices.[11] God's integrity confronts any and all lack of integrity in our own selves. Our instinctive response is to resist. John mentions three principal ways by which we try to avoid or push back; they are well summarized by the authors Francis Kelly Nemeck and Marie Theresa Coombs:[12] (1) Heightened desires for pleasures, whether they be sexual or excessive eating and drinking, excessive TV watching, living in a vicarious world of sports, porn, or taking a narcotic, in order to gain immediate relief from the spiritual and psychological distress God's initiatives provoke in us. (2) Getting angry and impatient, especially toward God but also toward others as well; ignoring or challenging God, bargaining with and complaining to God: "Why are you doing this to me?" "Will you ever stop this?" "What did I do to deserve this?" "I know what you are doing to me; just get it over with, damn it!" (3) Experiencing confusion, wondering what is going on with this distressing time, wanting an explanation but getting none, getting anxious over feeling out of control, of not knowing the meaning of all of this. Sometimes we might fear being psychologically sick or imagine our being terminally ill thanks to some hidden illness. There may actually be some psychosomatic problems that burden us while suffering in our soul. This provoking action of God is meant to enable us to "curb and bridle" our passions or be purged radically in our senses and spirit, where the roots of our disordered desires and the seven capital sins are found.

Some Examples

This process can remind us of the sufferings of Job or the prophet Jonah's experience in the belly of the whale.[13] It can be likened to Jesus's Gethsemane experience or the prophet Jeremiah's intense trials. Some are left feeling utterly abandoned by God and find little or no consolation in people and nature. They can be brought so close to the fire of God that they feel intensely the least thing in themselves that is not godly; they keenly feel their sin and spiritual misery, how wretched in soul they are while they fear that God has rejected them and they feel forsaken by friends and despised by others. Their deepest suffering is the anguish of fearing they have been abandoned by God. The book of Lamentations in the Old Testament describes well these sufferings. So too the account of St. Thérèse of Lisieux (d. 1897), the Carmelite Little Flower of France, who, while dying of tuberculosis, experienced in the last six months of her life strong temptations to think that there was nothing at all after one dies, that there is no God and that she would cease existing.

It is also exemplified with great drama in the life of Walter Ciszek, an American Jesuit priest (d. 1984). Imprisoned in Russia during World War II, Ciszek was interrogated daily by a Soviet KGB agent who pressured him for nearly three years to sign a confession that he was a spy. Ciszek resisted for all that time, until one day he broke under the constant mental pressure and signed the document. Moments after signing the confession Ciszek went into a rage against God for allegedly allowing him to fail him. He then experienced a loneliness and forsakenness that seemed infinite. It turned out to be a death to his own sense of the kind of priest he thought God wanted him to be. He called this his purgatory.[14] Soon afterward Ciszek was visited by a strong sense of God's presence and an inner light that changed the rest of his life. This opened him to a profound spiritual freedom through a complete surrender of himself to God and God's ways in each moment of the rest of his life. This gift of freedom would sustain him in some precarious and harrowing instances for the remaining nineteen years he was in Russia. In 1963 he was freed to return to the United States. God's grace opened Ciszek to new depths, enabling him to live with the habit of surrendering or abandoning himself to God in each moment of his day. Like St. Paul, he could now say more than ever, "I live, no longer I, but Christ lives in me" (Gal 2:20)!

It needs to be said that there are similar examples in the lives of each of us. There are those single parents and married couples whose service or, better, ministry to each other and to their children can expose them to much suffering and inner purification of motivation in order to be true to God and their vows, to the life they have generated, and to their own true selves. So too those who suffer loss of work or loss of home, major financial loss, life-threatening sickness, or live with the memories of abuse of one kind or another. Through such trials we can undergo deep spiritual transformation, often not recognized for what it is, if we respond to our situation with courageous faith and hope in God.

In the most severe experiences of this darkness, in what John of the Cross calls the dark night of the spirit, the "inflow of God" can bring to light not only the evils of our soul but also a profound knowledge of the infinite holiness and otherness of God. This deeper illumination can leave one tempted to despair of ever again coming into the graces of God, so contrary to God does one feel. The pain can be so heavy that such people can hardly pray vocally but can only put their face to the ground in profound humility and wait on God to lift them up, if God would be so gracious to do so. It makes those who suffer this way to forget past blessings, as if they were unreal, and leaves them feeling like God is even opposed to them. But the truth is that they are "hidden in God"[15] through this soul-searing, foundation-shaking process.

I have known some of this pain in my own life and know relatives who have been in this state, even though I am not certain whether they have understood the spiritual significance of their situation. My own experience hints to me that this deep soul-work by God is far more common in and around us than we usually recognize. What we carry within and what is unfolding there is so profound and very beautiful. Nothing in the human journey is just ordinary; all is extraordinary.

Finishing This Purification Process

When God finishes with us in this process, we experience ourselves being swept up into God. There is unleashed from within our depths a passionate, burning love for God. As with Fr. Ciszek, all the energies of our soul are united, focused, and intensely concentrated. This process releases tremendous longings and makes us bold and relentless in our quest for God. But it can exhaust us as well. So much of what we valued before comes to mean much less or is even worthless. Our many desires have been greatly simplified so that, in the end, we have one and only one desire for ourselves and for every other creature: total union with God and with everyone and everything united in God. It is so powerful to feel the impact of this process coming to a climax, to a wondrous integration. John of the Cross likens the process to the efforts of a blacksmith bending and shaping iron through sustained, intense fire to create something very beautiful.[16] Yes, the dark night in its deeper phases can feel violent to the human person; the hand of God can feel oppressive. Yet the person chosen by God for such deep transformation radiates with Divinity, the deepest reality of every human being. Many may think that a process so intense and deep is for the rare human being. It is true that since the process is largely hidden it is impossible to estimate confidently how numerous are those taken by God on this side of death into the deepest phases of this process. But studying what happens in those whom God does choose for the most challenging parts of the process allows us to have some sense of what God will do in each of us before our own process is complete and we come into his presence face to face. If contraries cannot coexist, as John of the Cross repeatedly insists, then God must somehow complete the purification process in every one of us before we come to the end of our journey into him . . . whether on this side or the other side of death. There cannot be the least condition of ungodliness in us before coming into final union with him and his saints.

God's infinite love and unending reverence for us accomplishes this miracle of transformation in beauty, truth, and goodness, and brings us into Christ's freedom.

Jesus has done much for us to make possible our salvation and transformation in God. But there is something further for us to recognize in him. He shows us something about ourselves as human beings and reveals to us the kind of God that God is. These two insights will greatly enhance our awareness of how great is the beauty of our transformation in Christ. Let us now explore this.

Questions for Discussion and Faith-Sharing

1. In what ways have you experienced being powerless, out of control, and having to surrender, to depend and wait? Have you experienced God's strength at such times?

2. Have you experienced being attracted to a more contemplative (wordless, image-less) prayer, of simply being and resting in God's presence? What is that like for you?

3. Which of the three "storms and trials" described above have you gone through?

4. Cite people you know about who have lived something of the dark night process. Describe a little of their situation and something of the blessings from it.

5. Find the paintings of Sieger Koder that depict the suffering, crucified Christ. Ponder any of them closely. Or, read and reflect on the book of Job and/or the book of Lamentations for powerful descriptions and images of human suffering. Share on this.

Chapter Seven

JESUS REVEALS GOD AND HUMANITY

To be human is to be vulnerable and suffer, to lose and not to have control over many factors in life. Ultimately it is to die. This we reflected on in the previous chapter. In this chapter I wish to consider some unique perspectives that Jesus's humanity and divinity bring to the meaning of our Passover journey.

The Human Self Jesus Shows Us

History demonstrates that the passion of Jesus is the most powerful source for Christians to find the strength they need in their encounters with vulnerability, dependence, and suffering. So many are drawn to this One who, out of love, hung on the cross for them and everyone else (John 12:32). At the cross they sense with him a communion in understanding and love, and a strength to go on with their lives. They may be sharing in his humiliation, in his loss and dying, yet they experience a spiritual power projected from the cross that offers them hope against all odds (John 3:14-16). They encounter a God who embraces the human condition, even the worst of what can happen to a human being. At the same time this God reveals to the world divine mercy and love that overcome darkness of spirit, injustice, and death. In Christ God faces this situation squarely and assures us of the way through it and beyond it.

While we appreciate in Jesus the best of all human possibilities, his dying experience demonstrates our frightful inability to avoid suffering, failure, rejection, and death. Our "godforsakenness" is reflected in Jesus's dying as a criminal and feeling completely abandoned by God.[1] These dimensions of his dying are an inescapable part of being human. Much of human history and its sins can be traced back to a fear of our vulnerabilities and mortality. This is demonstrated in our choosing often to live out of the illusion that we can take care of ourselves; that we are self-sufficient, self-justifying, and have control of our lives, even control over death. In many ways we want to "go it alone," to be gods like the first humans wanted to be (Gen 3:5). We can be especially attracted to live out of the values of the Standard of Satan, as explained in chapter 5. Jesus, however, tells us to have courage and not be afraid, that is, not to let fear blind us to his love. He offers us from his own experience a spiritual bond with Abba Father strong enough to survive betrayal, the feelings of abandonment, or any other loss or danger we might have to suffer when going through the valley of darkness.

In Jesus we are offered the way to a peace the world cannot give, to a freedom from the fear of our innate powerlessness. In him God shares all the bitterness that goes with being human; he enters into it all so that we will never be alone when forces beyond our control take us there. Saint Paul speaks to this choice of God to be with us in this radical poverty when he writes to the Corinthians, "for your sake he [Jesus] became poor although he was rich, so that by his poverty you might become rich" (2 Cor 8:9). God, then, gives us more than just comfort and reassurance. Rather, in Jesus God becomes one of us so that he may lift us beyond the powers of death and strengthen us against all the ways we might betray our deeper selves when trying to evade death. In doing this he, the Good Shepherd, leads us to eternal life.

God's saving power is a consequence of his self-emptying love manifest in Jesus. As the Persons within the triune God do, pouring out themselves completely to each other, Jesus does the same at Calvary, pouring out himself completely to the Father and to us. He does this so that we, his brothers and sisters, will be transformed in God's own time into a way of being in which we will live and love with the same unreserved depth that he lives and loves. We will relate to each other and all creation as the triune God does, in total, unconditional truth and love, giving and receiving without reservation. How exquisitely beautiful this transformation going on in us!

The God Jesus Shows Us

There is greater beauty for us to observe, however, when we consider the kind of God that is revealed at Calvary. At first glance there seems to be nothing beautiful about Jesus's situation at Calvary. We do not want to look at the God shown to us there, helpless in the midst of a terrible dying experience (Isa 52:2-3). This is not the kind of God anyone would expect or want. No one would ever invent a religion with this scene as the climax of God's coming into the world. Christian theologians for much of our two-thousand-year history have been rather constrained or totally ignored talking about God as powerless. It is, however, a perspective on God that comes from the Bible, especially in the stories of the prophets and of Jesus. At Calvary we see a God who is humiliated and vulnerable, broken and beaten, victimized by great injustice and betrayal. This is a God who has chosen to identify with us and is available to us in all our sufferings. We have to ask, Has there ever been a love like this? Or compassion like this?

The world and Christians in general, however, do not want this kind of God. For God to be vulnerable suggests the possibility of our losing many of our dreams, our security and control. This would even hint that in the end evil prevails over truth and goodness. In many ways we do not believe in this kind of God because we sense that to believe this would mean we would have to live our life with similar vulnerability and selfless generosity. It would mean our having to accept and live in fidelity to the truth of our human condition as poor and in radical need of God's saving actions. We much prefer a God who is victorious and powerful, a king seated in triumph on his throne guaranteeing us security, pleasures, and a long life.

When we let the shocking revelation of this kind of God sink into our consciousness, we meet God like never before. When we stand unprotected before Christ on the cross who loves unto folly, when we surrender to this love, we experience God like never before. Not only do we begin to be healed of our fears and pride; not only do we begin to be freed from our anger at God for letting life be so difficult, harsh, and unjust. We are also, amazingly, moved to want to love God and all of creation with something of the same kind of abandon. We begin to understand this kind of love, the beauty of it; we do not confuse it with a misguided masochism; instead, it truly makes sense to our hearts. Consequently, we desire to give ourselves as "fools for Christ" and love God and others with the same kind of humility, nonviolence, and total outpouring as seen in Jesus.[2]

The hope that emerges from our souls, then, is boundless. We have hope for ourselves, for all our loved ones, even for all the most forlorn and desperate of the world. Somehow we know in the deepest parts of ourselves that this love will have the final say in everything, that his mercy is infinite. It extends even to the perpetrators, the victimizers, and all of us who wittingly or unwittingly continue to crucify our neighbor, the Body of Christ. To look intently and deeply into the eyes of this God-Man hanging on the cross can change forever the way we understand God and the human person, our neighbor, and ourselves. To contemplate this crucified One can eventually move us to desire to share in all aspects of his life. We will want to live with him one shared life, to know and love him, even to be like him, in every respect. No one opens up our soul with its beauty and possibilities as does he and the beauty of his Heart, in the way and to the extent he loves. No one!

The truth of a vulnerable God and the truth of our human reality as shown on the cross are difficult to accept, but there is no other way to our becoming who we are destined to be. God has chosen poverty as the way for saving the world. It is God's way, the way of humility, for divinizing us. Only when experiencing God's unconditional love manifest in Christ can we embrace this truth as the wisdom of God, what the world rejects as foolishness. As we come to trust God's way, truth, and life in Jesus, we become increasingly an image of God, with the face of Christ being sketched by the Spirit-Paraclete in greater and greater detail in our depths. We become more human and alive in Christ. We are allowing God's Spirit to reign in us, with no other power coercing or hindering us from living in God's freedom. The beauty of God increasingly shines through our person, thanks to God's faithful work of transforming us in Christ. This does not necessarily mean we are walking "saints," but it does mean that God has given birth in our soul to very noble desires and opened us to grow to significant holiness. In time, if we allow, God will enable us to realize these great longings and to live habitually from them.

In the meantime there is a great probability that we will die with many things unresolved in our lives. There could be deep in us, maybe unconscious to us, attitudes that constitute our saying no to God in certain aspects of our lives. "I [am] refus[ing] to be a creature—not in general, but in this attitude, that relation[ship]; this habit, that attachment. I find that I have not been able to say the yes [to some particularities even though I have been moved to offer everything in general]." Therefore "I will so dispose myself . . . that God my Lord can say that yes in me, and say all those little yeses that I have wanted to say and have not been able to say. I will wait upon the Lord. If with humankind it is impossible—with God all things are possible."[3]

To have discovered God as the greatest "find" of our life, as the pearl of inestimable value, and to desire to give ourselves completely, unconditionally, to God is, however, the beginning of our receiving the fullness of such a singular grace. God wants this for us much more than we do, and he will—with our consent—overcome in us any and every obstacle until we receive this blessing.

Conclusion and Transition

We have looked at human powerlessness and Divinity manifest in vulnerability. We reflected on how humanity has a radical need for God and how unconditional is God's gift of himself to meet our need. As previously indicated this reflection has given us a glimpse of God as well, and, in that glimpse, has given us a hint of what we will be like, thanks to the transformation in Christ that is happening in ourselves. It is my primary interest in this book to address this theme at some length: what we will "look" like when fully transformed, divinized, and brought completely into this new self. The final two chapters will focus on this, first looking at the individual person and then at the human race.

Questions for Discussion and Faith-Sharing

1. Name someone in your life, past or present, who has helped you gain some noteworthy sense of what God "looks" like by your knowing him or her. What specifically in that person has reflected for you a trait or quality of God?

2. Have you been around a person who in great suffering has manifested something of the love and peace, forgiveness and trust in God that Jesus showed in his passion and dying? What was that like for you? Has it helped you

appreciate the story of Jesus's passion in new ways or with new awareness? How so?

3. How do you reconcile God's vulnerability with God's power? Briefly explain.

4. Of all the qualities highlighted in this chapter about the kind of love manifest in Jesus humiliated and crucified, and the kind of love manifest in God as vulnerable, which ones mean the most to you when considering that both Jesus and God are showing us qualities that will be characteristic of us in our transformed, heavenly state?

Chapter Eight

MORE THAN YOU COULD EVER IMAGINE

This chapter provides an intuitive way, through poetic images, for gaining insight into what the transformed, divinized human person will be like at the end of his or her Passover journey. All of these images come from Spain's greatest religious poet, St. John of the Cross, a sixteenth-century Carmelite priest (d. 1591). One is found in his book *The Dark Night*. All the others come from his book *The Living Flame of Love*, which consists of a poem of four stanzas and his explication of the poem. Each image offers us a new perspective on this great mystery. Readers will find certain ones more helpful, more appealing than others, but together St. John is offering something to everyone.

The Log on a Fire

Probably his most memorable image for describing the process of our spiritual transformation is that of a log of wood thrown on a fire.

Sitting at an outdoor campfire in the dark on a clear, cool summer evening makes for some pleasant memories. How many of us have sat there and watched during the passing minutes what happens to a large log as the fire begins to envelop and penetrate it? Saint John uses this metaphor to explain what happens to us as the Holy Spirit, called by John "the Living Flame of Love," transforms us in Christ. With fascinating detail John draws out the implications in this metaphor by highlighting various stages of fire penetrating a log. We are left to admire the artistry of God, freeing and re-creating us by bringing forth our potential for Divinity.

John says that, like the log being immersed more and more in the fire, we, as we progress on our Passover journey, are more and more taken into God. We are exposed to God's powerful action that purges us eventually of all that is ungodly, of all that is un-Christlike, and imparts to us divine light, new loving knowledge of God, of neighbor, of ourselves, and of all creation:

> Fire, when applied to wood, first dehumidifies it, dispelling all moisture and making it give off any water it contains. Then it gradually turns the wood black, makes it dark and ugly, and even causes it to emit a bad odor. By drying out the wood, the fire brings to light and expels all those ugly and dark accidents [elements] which are contrary to fire. Finally, by heating and enkindling it from without, the fire transforms the wood into itself and makes it as beautiful as it is itself. Once transformed, the wood no longer has any activity or passivity of its own, except for its weight and its quantity which is denser than the fire. For it possesses the properties and performs the actions of fire: it is dry and it dries; it is hot and it gives off heat; it is brilliant and it illumines; and it is also light, much lighter than before. It is the fire that produces all these properties in the wood.[1]

And marvelous to the eye, the wood, whose cross-section shows its concentric rings glowing, has now become the fire. The transformation is complete.

In a similar fashion, the action of this "Living Flame of Love" transforms each one of us. The beginnings of this process are not pleasant. St. John writes,

> Before transforming [our] soul, [the fire] purges it of all contrary qualities. It produces blackness and darkness and brings to the fore [our] soul's ugliness; thus [our] soul seems worse than before and unsightly and abominable. This divine purge stirs up all the foul and vicious humors [moods or dispositions] of which [our] soul was never before aware; never did [we] realize there was so much evil in itself, since these humors were so deeply rooted [and largely hidden]. And now that they may be expelled and annihilated they are brought to light and seen clearly through the illumination of this dark light of divine contemplation. Although [our] soul is no worse than before, neither in itself nor in its relationship with God, it feels undoubtedly so bad as to be not only unworthy that God should see [us] but deserving of His abhorrence; in fact, it feels that God now does abhor [us].[2]

How sobering this process. It can entail significant suffering of various kinds. While the divine fire itself is gentle, the experience of our being transformed by this loving light and wisdom can be painful. We are rather weak and burdened with numerous imperfections. In various ways, conscious and unconscious, we are attached to so many things: our status, our reputation, our financial security, possibly even the way we have been praying or the way we image God and ourselves. We resist giving up control and the changes that come with it. Such are the contraries that cannot coexist peacefully with God, "just as the log of wood until prepared cannot be transformed by the fire that is applied to it."[3] When there are in our lives behaviors reflecting pride or envy, anger or lust, greed, sloth or gluttony, it will be painful for us to encounter the presence and purity of God. There will ensue a war of great contraries raging inside us. Virtues and imperfections will be at odds with each other. One will try to expel the other because contraries cannot coexist. "One contrary when close to the other makes it more manifest."[4] However, once these imperfections and bad habits are purged, sometimes over months and even years in our lives, our sufferings come to an end and joy prevails. This is not just as an absence of pain, because now there is a significant communion of likenesses with God, and we have become much more free.

Yet this is hardly the end of God's initiated holy, demanding process. There is more for God's Spirit to bring forth in us. The divine fire penetrates further, becomes more intense and all pervasive. Again, it acts like fire in the wood and penetrates closer to the center of the log. It makes the wood hotter and prepares it for complete transformation. In other words, after a purification of the more exterior imperfections, for example, of certain behaviors, this living flame of divine love focuses on our more interior imperfections. These will be attitudes and long-held dispositions or unconscious values. God, the loving flame, will purify us of such and bring us more completely into harmony with the Heart and Spirit of God. This deeper purification will mean even greater suffering than what we experienced when we were being freed from our more exterior imperfections. John says that when God touches these core disorders in us with the fire of his uncompromising love, we experience nothing but our own spiritual bitterness. We see like never before how unlike God we are and how desperately we need God's healing. We can feel so unfit for God, so far away from realizing our deepest spiritual hopes. "The suffering of the soul becomes more intimate, subtle, and spiritual in proportion to the inwardness, subtlety, spirituality, and deep-rootedness of the imperfections which are removed."[5] God can go deeply and do much in a very short time, yet for some this process can be drawn out over months and even years.

What, then, becomes of us as we approach the close of this transformation process? What will we "look like" when God finishes with us, when we are penetrated with the divine fire, and, like the log becoming fire in its final state, we become divine? This is an outcome that is so wondrously beautiful! It is something of what Jesus knew in his Heart and that moved him from his depths to give his all for us. This ultimate purpose of God is spoken of in the gospels, proclaimed extensively in the letters of St. Paul, and reflected on with joyous wonder by numerous men and women Christian mystics throughout the centuries.

The essence of this glorious news is the frequently invoked saying of the Fathers of the Greek-speaking Eastern Christian church: *the Divine became human so that the human may become Divine.* God became one of us, truly and fully human, so that we might become gods, fully human and truly divine. But what does it mean for us to become divine? It sounds so preposterous! It might even sound arrogant for us to speak this way. It could be another version of the trap that the original human beings fell prey to when they consented to eat the forbidden fruit in the Garden of Eden. And then too, many of us have rather deficient ideas of what constitutes Divinity, of who God is.

John of the Cross leads us in our reflections on this most exalted theme. His writings on this are considered by many as the most developed and beautiful explanation of what we human beings will be and act like in the next life. He is of the opinion that God brings very few people to complete transformation before death. He is in complete accord with the church's teachings regarding the purgatorial process of transformation we must go through to reach our divine destiny. This process, as he understands it, begins in our earliest years, continues throughout our life, and for the majority of us is completed in the next life. But it is worth our while to look closely with St. John at the lives of those who are fully transformed while still in this life and are blessed with what we can call a hint of the heavenly life and gain a significant sense of the glorious destiny that awaits us.

Great Likeness to God

Like the log of wood permeated with fire and transformed into fire, St. John sees the transformed human being living the life of God, doing what God does, knowing what God knows, and loving as God loves. This is the full realization of our baptism and all other sacramental moments in our life. We come to live forever in this glorious fire of divine love. Everything we do—in thought, memory, or act of will and choice—is a divine act and yet it is still our own act. John likens these acts to flames flaring up on the transformed log. God initiates and produces these acts in complete freedom, with no spiritual contraries inhibiting his actions. They are particular expressions of this amazing union we will enjoy with God. John says that in such moments these people of God's special providence think they are being given eternal life. It is like they have died and fallen into God's arms, so lifted up into God are they. They can do only what is proper to God, so completely at one are they with God and all God loves. One can hardly imagine the freedom God enjoys in the souls of such people!

Such exceptional people are in God and God in them, completely. God and they live one shared life, completely one in spirit. We can meaningfully say that such people feel what God feels, rejoice in what God rejoices in, and weep over what God weeps about. Since they are so raised up to the actions of God in God, they are given a profound foretaste of eternal life (2 Cor 12:1-6, esp. v. 4). Their most earnest prayer is for this spiritual betrothal, as St. John calls it, to be ended and the eternal spiritual marriage to begin. They live with immense hope in the One to whom they are betrothed. And they trust God's wisdom about when it will be best for him to take them home. But, despite this extraordinary experience of union, while in this life they still have to tend to ordinary daily affairs as the rest of us do. Such highly favored people can be those with major responsibilities and demands for leadership and care of people, innovators and founders of movements God has inspired for conversion, reformation, and healing (*Living Flame of Love*, st. II, sec. 12). Well-known examples of such people are Sts. Bonaventure, Bernard of Clairvaux, Catherine of Siena, Thérèse of Lisieux, Padre Pio; Sr. Mary Ward; and Mother Teresa of Calcutta.

But surely there are some people blessed with this gift of transformation who live lives that appear to be much more ordinary. It can be said they are more "hidden in God." They might live alone, be widowed or divorced, or struggle to care for their family. They might live with some disability and have to depend greatly on the help of others. They are the type whom the Bible calls God's *anawim* or "little ones."

Whether publicly known or hidden, these people are so given to God in this world through love and service simply because their sole occupation at this highest level of transformation before death is simply to receive God. The eye of their soul is steadily fixed on the one love of their life. They are so yielded to God, so sensitive to the least wish of God that their joy is to be touched by what John calls the "wounds" of divine love. God so enjoys engaging with them in what John calls the joyous and festive arts or games of love. Deeper and deeper are these "wounds" in the person's soul, eventually to the deepest center of the person's soul—like the fire penetrating to the center of the log—until the soul appears to be God. Yes, appears to be God! And how can this be so?

A Crystal Shining with Light

One might ask, how can a creature like us be brought to a state so as to appear as the Creator? Saint John has an interesting reply; he says that God has so given himself to the person, so transformed the soul of this man or woman that his or her soul is like a crystal, clean and pure, on which light shines. This new image offers us another perspective on what we are destined to be. The more intense the light, the brighter becomes the crystal.

If you increase the light enough, the crystal will appear indistinguishable from the light, so filled with light is it (ibid., st. I, sec. 13). So too once the presence and transformation of God is complete in us, we will appear as God. Each and every person God has created is invited into this transformation. Too often, however, we are afraid of God's initiatives and where they will take us. We do not let this process go forward. Or, we do not receive competent guidance and reassurance and, therefore, are not able to capitalize on these extraordinary opportunities of God's grace. Or, as St. John says, the Evil One can divert us by attracting us back to what is sensibly pleasurable in earlier kinds of prayer and earlier, less challenging stages of the spiritual life (st. III, sec. 29–67).[6]

But for those who do allow God to lead and, if available, receive guidance during these experiences of darkness and purification, the miracle of transformation unfolds and the Spirit-Paraclete radically changes their person and life.

Once God has entered into and transformed this deepest part of us, no further transformation is necessary. All that awaits us is our dying and entering eternal life, where these "arts and games of love" between God and us will go on forever.

John anticipates those who are tempted to dismiss this vision of our coming life as exaggerated, as wishful thinking, by appealing to the utter goodness and generosity of God. He describes God as the "Father of lights [Jas 1:17], who is not close-fisted but diffuses Himself abundantly, as the sun does its rays, without being a respecter of persons [Acts 10:34], wherever there is room—always showing Himself gladly along the highways and byways—[and] does not hesitate or consider it of little import to find His delights with the children of men at a common table in the world [Prov 8:31]" (st. I, sec. 15).

John continues in responding to those who are dubious about such divine generosity: "It should not be held as incredible in a soul now examined, purged, and tried in the fire of tribulations, trials, and many kinds of temptations, and found faithful in love, that the promise of the Son of God be fulfilled, the promise that the [Father and Son] will come and dwell within anyone who loves Him [John 14:23]. The Blessed Trinity inhabits the soul by divinely illumining its intellect with the wisdom of the Son, delighting its will in the Holy Spirit, and by absorbing it powerfully and mightily in the delightful embrace of the Father's sweetness" (ibid.). These acts of the intellect and the will, our soul's functions for knowing and making choices, are the two actions most distinctive of divine life, the life of the triune God. Through such profound transformation, thanks to a God whose generosity is more than could ever be imagined, our knowing and willing are made to be nothing less than divine acts. We live the life of God, so transformed in God are we. The life of God that was given to us at our baptism, like a tiny seed, has now come to full flowering and endless fruitfulness. This is the state of life that will be ours forever, in perpetual giving and receiving with God and with those in the communion of saints: in knowing and being known, in loving and being loved, in continuous and total mutuality. How overwhelming!

There are those of us who have been blessed to know the joys and riches of faithful, unconditional friendship. Others experience long-term married love, with the sharing together in all that goes with good times and bad times. Gifts from God like these are the perfect, divinely providential preparation for the ultimate gift of himself. They can stir in us, as well, longings for the fullness of union with all that we have come to love, human and nonhuman. They ready us for eternal friendship and love, the complete giving of ourselves to these others, to God, and to all who are in complete union with God.

But those who are still self-centered and fear- and/or pride-based in their manner of relating are too distracted, too blind to be drawn to this joyous destiny. They are like the log that is still damp and cold with respect to the divine flame. The deep purgatorial initiatives of God still await them, whether in this life or, if they so choose, in the next life where there is no procrastinating, no avoiding, no hiding from the truth of our spiritual state.

A Cautery

Besides the metaphors of the log and the crystal, John of the Cross has us look at a third image to give us insight into the awesome transformation of our person. It gives us some sense of the miracles of love we will be empowered to do. It is the image of a cautery or branding iron used to sear and disinfect flesh. The iron is shaped like that of a pencil, comes to a point, and allows precise and delicate touches by a surgeon. John develops his image by first describing the Holy Spirit as a cautery because he refers to the Lord, while quoting the book of Deuteronomy, as a "consuming fire," a fire of love that can "consume and transform into itself the soul it touches." In certain cases the touches of the divine surgeon can be rather vehement, seeming to the person to be hotter than all the other fires on earth. For this reason the person "calls the Holy Spirit a cautery" (st. II, sec. 2). He or she also calls "the *act* of this union a cautery" (st. II, sec. 2–3) since it produces an effect more singular than any other fire, an act of the Holy Spirit more transforming than any other action in the soul. It is "the outcome of a fire so much more aflame than all the others." And finally, because the soul is entirely transformed by the divine flame, it itself "has become a cautery of blazing fire" (st. II, sec. 2). Wonder of wonders, it is not consumed or destroyed by this divine fire, nor is it afflicted by it; rather, it is divinized, exalted, enlarged, brightened, and filled with delight. God's manner, despite the power of his love capable of overwhelming us as fragile creatures, is most gentle and sweet with the person. It is said that the soul of such a rare person is consumed in the immense glory of God. This person "knows all things, tastes all things, does all it wishes, and prospers; no one prevails before it and nothing touches it" (st. II, sec. 4). Such a person enjoys the greatest possible welcome of God and a sharing in all the goods and secrets of God's wisdom.

As a cautery of love the Holy Spirit "wounds," while healing and curing miseries and sins as it wounds. These wounds or divine touches, in turn, become wounds of love in that God in his providence has turned them to good. They might have been an occasion for one's having been humbled and opened up to God, saved for something providential and freed for new apostolic possibilities. John says such a person, so taken up into divine love, now sees all of creation penetrated by this love; the entire cosmos has become a sea of love that engulfs the person and everything around him or her. This person, understandably, overflows with gratitude, praise, and the joy of the Holy Spirit. He or she "finds God in all things," as St. Ignatius of Loyola would say, and "the soul [of the person] is converted into the immense fire of love which emanates from [the] enkindled point at the heart of [his or her] spirit" (st. II, sec. 11). In certain special cases these woundings of love can extend even to their bodies, as it did for St. Francis of Assisi (d. 1226), St. Catherine of Siena (d. 1380), and St. Padre Pio (d. 1968) as well as for other people, some in our own times who bear the wounds of Jesus, called the stigmata. Painful for their bodies, these physical wounds are cause for enormous delight in their spirit. Their sense of communion with God is indescribable.

Yet more wondrous than what happens to our bodies is what happens in our souls. What is so wondrous is that we come to know by another, higher way. This is a way that bypasses our usual ways of knowing through our five senses and gives us an immediate knowledge of God, of one another, and of all that God has created. It is an infinite and astounding expansion of our knowing. We will see as God sees and know as God knows!

And there are further wonders. We will love with the Heart and affection of God. The Holy Spirit will be so full in us, like the fire permeating completely the log of wood, giving us divine strength to live this new and eternal life of loving as only God can love. Our memory will be transformed such that it will be the memory of God. That is, we will have the span of God's way of seeing: beyond the limits of time and aware of each creature in terms of its eternal significance. What delights God will be that which delights us. What is truthful and good will draw us into God, like metal filing drawn by a magnet. But that which is beautiful will especially pull us close to God. We will gaze in wonder at the One who is Beauty himself, enjoying his Presence in all things, and be filled with awe at how all things are in him, in Beauty. No wonder, then, we will have no interest in or inclination to anything not harmonious with God. Our only joy and freedom will be in living the life of God and God living our life. In this one transformative, divinizing process each of us will have realized fully our potential for Divinity. All of us together will be brought into one communion in Christ, as a new creation in God, when God will be All in all (1 Cor 15:28).

Truly, God is the great and consummate artist. He fashions such a re-creation and brings us all in Christ to an astounding destiny. He changes death to life and our animal life to spiritual life. All the movements, operations, and inclinations of our soul had previously been subject to competing, contrary forces, making the operations of our soul in one degree or another like the scattered light rays of normal light. God's presence in Christ realigns all of these movements. He is like a special lens realigning scattered light rays and drawing them together to be a laser with all the rays moving in one direction. In a similar way God performs an even greater wonder by reclaiming and redirecting all of our soul's energies that previously were oriented to death and eternal unhappiness. John of the Cross exults at such a glorious deed when he praises God: "In killing you changed death to life" (*Living Flame of Love*, st. II, sec. 32–34, esp. 34). This would be like saying, "In doing to death all of these chaotic, misdirected uses of the God-given energies of my soul and body, and in reclaiming what has been blindly and hopelessly used by me, you, God, redeem me and bring me to life. You are my Savior and that of the entire world!"

It is good to remind ourselves that John is looking at the soul of a person already transformed while still in this earthly life. We are reflecting on this in order to ponder something of the holy, eternal mystery unfolding in our own selves and in any and all who aspire to live in Christ. We may be seeking him consciously, baptized into his life and living through faith in his continuous resurrected presence. Or we might be relating to him in veiled, hidden, or even unknown ways, for example, in our relating to our neighbor, in nature, and through non-Christian religious pathways. Regardless, anyone seeking to live in fidelity to the Truth, as in God's providence they have recognized this Truth, is living in Christ and is being embraced by this Sacred Mystery, the Source of everything that exists. This vision of transformation in God, then, applies to each and to all throughout history, in all cultures, in every religion, and wherever there is the seeking of this Truth with goodwill.

Lamps of Fire

Saint John, as if he has not already overwhelmed us with his vision of what we will become in Christ, gives us another image. In this instance it is as if he puts the human soul under a microscope and highlights for us how, in the person fully transformed in Christ, all of the attributes of God are found. In his wonderfully poetic way John calls these attributes "lamps of fire." He emphasizes that, while we may *have* these various attributes, for example, mercy and truth, wisdom and goodness, God *is* each of these attributes. God *is* mercy, *is* truth, *is* wisdom, *is* omnipotence, *is* beauty, and so forth. And God lives and acts with complete freedom within the soul of such a person—as mercy, as wisdom, as any one of these dimensions we experience God to be. For example, God loves me in my garden where I find so much creativity and peace; there he reveals himself as beauty. Sometimes God loves me through his faithfulness and protection in situations where I overstep my abilities or imprudently risk; there God reveals himself as truth. God will love me at times in an experience of reconciliation with another person and reveal himself as mercy. These attributes or lamps of fire, then, are found in the human soul of any person who enjoys this profound union with God. John of the Cross depicts God thus saying to the soul of such a transformed person, "I am yours and for you and delighted to be what I am so as to be yours and give myself to you" (st. III, sec. 6).

Like any lamp that is lit, giving off light and heat, we, once transformed in God, will also give forth light and heat. Each attribute, which is God, will enlighten our soul and transmit the warmth of divine love. God will enlighten us with knowledge of himself, transmit his love, and we in turn will witness to all creation this profound knowledge and love of God. We will find ourselves living within what John calls "the splendors" or "over-shadowings" of these lamps (st. III, sec. 9–12, 12–13). Then the joy and victory of God will shine out, plainly manifest in our personal history: both in the struggles, crosses, and wounds of our lives as well as in our choices, labors, and successes for God's kingdom.

A Well of Living Waters

Then still another image, this one softer or less intense than the previous ones. John says the soul of anyone completely trans-formed by God overflows with joy at being so loved by God and thus is said to be "flooded with divine waters" (st. III, sec. 8). In turn the soul is said to be like a well of living waters, giving life, giving God, just as God its origin does. He or she has died to all self-centeredness, to all contraries, and is now doing divine acts. The Spirit of God, "hidden in the veins of the soul" says John, is like "soft refreshing water, which satisfies the thirst of the [person's] spirit." Insofar as the Spirit is active, manifesting deeds of love through the transformed person, it is like "living flames of fire" (ibid.).[7] This great gift of God comes to abide in us and transforms us in himself. Such a revelation is the best part of the Good News of Jesus Christ.

After trying to give us some sense of our spiritual future, John of the Cross surrenders and admits, "All that can be said of [this mystery] is less than the reality, for the transformation of the soul in God is indescribable" (ibid.).

We Become Divine

While humbling himself before this Mystery of Love, John proceeds to reflect for us on the most profound implications of this mystery he has wanted to show us. He says that "the soul becomes God from God through participation in Him and in His attributes, . . . the 'lamps of fire' " (ibid.; also st. III, sec. 78). The soul becomes *God*, John says! This shocking statement moves the saint to share the most beautiful part of his vision.

John takes us deeper, this time into the interior of the soul and its various operations of remembering, understanding, and willing or choosing. He images them as *"the deep caverns of feeling"* (st. III, sec. 18), implying how infinitely deep is their capacity for receiving and relating to God. It is most specifically in these depths that we become God by participation in God. They are made by God for God. Nothing less than God will ever satisfy their longings. The various attachments we get burdened by in life keep us out of touch with these depths and dull our longings for the Holy. The transformed person, by contrast, freed from such disorders and superficial distractions, is drawn powerfully at his or her deepest center to complete union with God.

Perhaps we have met such people who are well on their way to such spiritual freedom. Perhaps we recognize something of this same holy process at work in our own selves. John of the Cross says it is usually toward the end of our own purgation and time of illumination in God, that is, during the passive night of the spirit, when we will experience this, if we do in this life. He adds that it is specifically in the caverns of feeling of our soul where we will experience significant spiritual suffering as we thirst, sometimes with agony, for God: our understanding aching for wisdom, our will aching for the fullness of love, our memory longing for the possession of God. This is the suffering of the betrothed human lover longing for the eternal marriage with God. Only our dying will end our waiting for this gift. In times past we were ignorant of things natural and supernatural and blind due to our sins. John says our condition was like that of one having cataracts on our eyes and seeing only in a clouded sense (st. III, sec. 70–75).

Relating as God's Equal

Such a transformation makes, then, for extraordinary conse-quences in the person's relationship with God and with the rest of creation. As was said above, these caverns or faculties of the person's memory, understanding, and will are filled with the attributes of God, the splendors of the lamps shining in them, and they in turn give to God these same splendors that they have received. Because of this freedom and ability to give back everything to the Beloved, the person now knows a joy beyond all joys. To be able to speak gratitude, thanksgiving, and loving praise to God with *infinite* expression and depth is to reflect complete fulfillment and transformation for this human being. This will be our deepest satisfaction, happiness, and joy: to give to God our whole selves, but now transformed and therefore worth infinitely more than we were in our pre-transformed state! Our new selves, transformed in God, have become divine, have become God through the overwhelming generosity and power of God. Now we are able to give back to God the only gift really worthy of God, namely, God! Just as in the life of the triune God, living in total, mutual self-giving love among Father, Son, and Spirit, we are now capable of living the divine life in total self-giving with God. How true it is what St. Paul says in 1 Corin-thians 2:9, 10: "What eye has not seen, and ear has not heard, / and what has not entered the human heart, / what God has prepared for those who love him, / this God has revealed to us through the Spirit." We are reminded as well of St. Paul's stirring declaration in Galatians 2:20 that those who choose to live in and be taken up into this transforming Mystery can say with St. Paul, "I live, *no longer I*, but Christ lives in me." Truly, this is more than we could have ever asked for or imagined!

John continues opening up further dimensions of this wondrous mystery of God's re-creating us; he says that the soul of the person remade in the divine fullness shares with God wisdom and goodness and every other attribute of God to the degree that God has shared the same with it:

> Although (the soul) is not God as perfectly as it will be in the next life, it is like the shadow of God. Being the shadow of God through this substantial transformation, it performs in this measure in God and through God what He through Himself does in it. For the will of the two is one will, and thus God's operation and the soul's are one. *Since God gives Himself with a free and gracious will, so too the soul . . . gives to God, God Himself in God. And this is a true and complete gift of the soul to God. . . . Having Him for its own, it can give Him and communicate Him to whomever it wishes.* Thus it gives Him to its Beloved, who is the very God who gave Himself to it. (st. III, sec. 78; emphasis mine)

And furthermore:

> A reciprocal love is thus actually formed between God and the soul, like the marriage union and surrender, in which the goods of both (the divine essence which each possesses freely by reason of the voluntary surrender between them) are possessed by both together. They say to each other what the Son of God spoke to the Father through St. John [the gospel writer]: . . . *All my goods are yours and yours are mine*, and I am glorified in them [John 17:10]. (st. III, sec. 79)

Can anything be more beautiful than a relationship of total mutuality, of complete sharing, forever and ever, just as in the life of the triune God? We will love God as only God could, and love each other and our own selves as only God could. This means we will love God not just "because He is generous, good, and glorious to [us], but [more so] . . . because He is all this in Himself essentially" (st. III, sec. 82). And we will love each other not just because of blood ties or for what we did for each other but especially for who we are in our deepest selves, with all our godly beauty, goodness, and truth.

Seeing as God Sees

Finally, St. John of the Cross describes the life of the transformed person still living in this world in terms of a gentle and loving awakening of God in the deepest part of his or her soul. God is said to "breathe" within the person, communicating goodness and glory as well as "swelling the person's heart" with delicate and tender inspirations of love. Thanks to such an intimate blessing, the person awakens to how creation glows or radiates and moves in harmony (st. IV, sec. 2–4). Caught up in God, all is now seen for what it is. All is now transvalued. Everything discloses the beauty of the person's being, power, and loveliness, as well as the root of his or her duration and life. Creation, then, is diaphanous, transparent to its core. It speaks of its Maker and the beauty of the Maker. As a result of such singular spiritual vision, the person comes to know creatures through God, as opposed to our usual way of knowing: knowing God through creatures (st. IV, sec. 5). He or she comes to know God as the root of all and, in a way never before known, all creation rooted in him, given and sustained by him. So this person is given "God's eyes," the divine way of seeing things. He or she sees God moving, governing, bestowing being, power, graces, and gifts upon all creatures. And the person sees what God is in himself and what he is in his creatures all in one view (st. IV, sec. 7). Such an awakening in the person is more an awakening of God, says St. John. It is God's profound communication to the soul of this special person, "the communication of God's excellence to the substance of the soul" (st. IV, sec. 4, 9–16). What the person experiences is an immense, powerful voice in his or her soul, what St. John calls "the voice of a multitude of excellences, of thousands of virtues in God, infinite in number. The soul is established in them, terribly and solidly set in array like an army . . ., and made gentle and charming with all the gentleness and charm of creatures" (st. IV, sec. 10).

If this, then, is the destiny of each of us in God, what is the destiny of the human race in God as one creation and the family of God? This I wish to address in our last chapter.

Questions for Discussion and Faith-Sharing

1. Which of the images of St. John of the Cross speak best to you in intuiting something of the transformation in Christ that God's Holy Spirit is working in you and others? What is it about the image(s) that attract you so?

2. Go to http://www.cathovenelles.fr/leglise/reliques -nouvelle-eglise/ and next to the brief statement on St. Margaret Mary Alacoque, click on the image of the Sacred Heart painted by Luc Barbier at the Chapel of the Visitation in Paray-le-Monial, France. Note its brilliant colors of red, orange, yellow, and especially white around the wounds. Together these colors depict the power of Christ's Divinity shining through, but particularly the white that hints at what is "behind" the human form. Contemplate this image for some minutes and particularly how this picture of the risen Christ reflects what we will become in our transformed state. Share with others what you experience, what you see when gazing at this piece of art.

3. See Caravaggio's painting of the doubting Thomas, the apostle, placing his finger in the open side of the risen

Christ. Note the stunned look on Thomas's face, the sensitivity of Jesus in his eyes and mouth, as well as his hand guiding the hand of Thomas.

Chapter Nine

AND THERE WILL BE ONE CHRIST

Can we speak meaningfully about what happens to us as a human race at the end of the human journey? What are we *as a people* to become at the end of time? In the Christian Scriptures St. Paul is the principal voice addressing this theme. We can take a lead from his stirring words in 1 Corinthians 15:28: "When [at the end of time] everything is subjected to him [Christ], then the Son himself will [also] be subjected to the one [the Father] who subjected everything to him, *so that God may be all in all*." We can take further insight from the words of St. Augustine (d. 430) that at the end of time *there will be one Christ loving himself*.[1]

The Second Vatican Council (1962–65) addressed this theme when speaking about the church and all creation, saying that the church "will receive its perfection only in the glory of heaven, when the time for the renewal of all things will have come (Acts 3:21). At that time, together with the human race, the universe itself, which is closely related to humanity and which through it attains its destiny, will be perfectly established in Christ" (*Lumen Gentium* 48).

The book of Revelation assures us that in this new creation, called the heavenly Jerusalem, God will dwell among us, wiping away every tear from our eyes; death shall be no more—no mourning, no crying, no pain anymore. All that will be in the past. A new, eternal harmony and fullness will prevail. Those "united with Christ" will form the community of the redeemed, the holy city of God, the Bride of the Lamb. The vision of God enjoyed inexhaustibly by those transformed in Christ will be the unending source of joy, peace, and communion with every other transformed person. Even the nonhuman parts of creation will be caught up in the new creation, sharing in this all-encompassing glorification (Rom 8:22).

The Unfolding of a New Creation

The body of a new human family, of even a new creation, then, is in the process of an unfolding that anticipates the coming of this new era in Christ. Any human effort, even of the most humble kind, that expresses truth and goodwill and seeks the better ordering of human society contributes to the coming of this new era. Whatever we do to give life, to nurture it and serve others will be part of this new creation but freed from any residue of self-centeredness, freed to be part of the new Christ. It can be said, then, that heaven will be the fullness of reality, not as an ethereal state some have imagined, but the transformed fullness of the original creation God placed us in. Heaven will be in continuity with the life God is giving us throughout our years in this earthly state. The Eternal to some degree is already in our possession. We walk with the Eternal in our depths, in our heart and soul, until that great day when we finally come home to God along with all those in union with God. To know our heavenly future, then, we need to recognize hints of this future in regular daily experience, especially in significant relationships with others on the same Passover journey.

Perhaps no one in modern times has developed these clues in the Christian tradition more than the twentieth-century French Jesuit and scientist Pierre Teilhard de Chardin (d. 1955). His ability to study and interpret the "fingerprints" of God's actions demonstrated especially in the fossil remains of plants, animals, and the human species has given a new thrust to our wonder about what God is preparing us for. He has done this while interfacing his scientific findings with a prayerful reading of the writings of St. Paul and their mystical insights into the risen, "cosmic Christ." What he finds when he goes back and forth between biblical revelation and these exciting sources of God's actions seen in creation has left many Christians breathless. They have been greatly stirred at the vision Teilhard offers for the end of history and the final coming of Christ and our fullness in him. Even many who are indifferent to religion or are self-declared agnostics, some of them being Teilhard's own professional colleagues, have been captivated by his writings. Let us, then, let Teilhard lead us while we ponder these clues of God. They are offered for our own consideration and prayer, subject, of course, to the Christian Scriptures and declared tradition and teachings of the Christian church over its twenty centuries.

Teilhard de Chardin's overarching premise and insight regarding the direction and final destiny of all creation, human and otherwise, is that everything is moving relentlessly through ever greater levels of complexity, ever greater degrees of consciousness, toward a wholeness or completeness that can be described only in terms of the mystery of Christ. In saying this he echoes St. Paul, who speaks about a "pleroma" or fullness of being and life that God in Christ is bringing forth in all creation (Col 2:9-10; 1:18; Eph 1:10; Phil 2:10-11; 3:21; Heb 2:5-8).

Teilhard sees that at the very source of all that exists and in the life cycle and unfolding of every living thing there is "an invincible power of love" animating and guiding history. This means that there is one universal process in which the cosmos "'has gradually been taking on light and fire . . ., until it has come to envelop [us] in one mass of luminosity, glowing from within . . . The purple flush of matter fading imperceptibly into the gold of spirit, to be lost finally in the incandescence of a personal universe.' " [2]

This quote reminds us of the picture referred to in the second discussion question at the end of the previous chapter. Also it makes us recall what St. John of the Cross images when describing the transformation of the individual—a log of wood being gradually penetrated by fire until it becomes fire. Yet, the quote could also be used to image the transformation of all creation, nonhuman as well as human. Teilhard, for his part, says his experience with the earth has taught him that there is going on now "the diaphany of the divine at the heart of a glowing universe, the divine radiating from the depths of matter a-flame" (ibid., xiv). All is being "Christified."

What is emerging, then, in this glorious transformation of creation is a single entity of Love called the cosmic Christ. With Jesus the Christ, we and all creation are being personally and socially united with Christ, in his role as center and goal of the universal process of creation. Life's process will climax and its cocoon shell will fall away. Individually and as the entire human race, we will "step out of our own narrow and finalized life . . . into God's life. Life in God . . . becomes an absolute miracle." [3]

Gently and gradually God's Spirit helps us awaken to this emerging divine cosmic process. This awakening begins in our encountering Christ, consciously or unconsciously. Once we choose to live for something other than just ourselves and our own security and pleasures, we know him and enter into this Mystery. Our knowing happens through relationships with creatures, especially with other human beings. This ultimate Reality is hidden in the fragility and poverty of our lives, in our stories with their joys and tears, celebrations and pains. It seems rather clear that most people do not know him before death except in this hidden, obscure way. But thanks to God's gift of faith, many do recognize this universally present Christ in their encounter with Jesus of Nazareth, and eventually in all of humanity and in all creation, as it is united to him. It is a joyous and wondrous knowing of him shining through the ordinariness of our day, through other people, through our own selves, through the animals, plants, and rocks, the planets, sun, and galaxies, the whole cosmos. In Christ, then, there is taking place an embodiment or enfleshment of a wondrous communion of the human and the Divine, of the temporal and the eternal.

In summary, then, we can say with Teilhard, "There is a heart in the world . . . and this heart is the Heart of Christ . . . This mystery has two stages: the centre of convergence [the universe concentrates in one centre] and the Christian centre [this centre is the Heart of Christ]."[4]

The New Cosmic Christ

The cosmic Christ is not some new being with a consequent loss of identity for the persons and other creatures making it up. Rather, each member's identity is brought to its fullness in this mystery of transformation. Nor is the cosmic Christ simply a gathering of all creatures in some loosely held bond or collective.

Instead, it is a new creation, and the historical Jesus—who at the same time is God's Son—is its firstborn. Those who have faith in him as Lord and Savior—whether a conscious faith lived out in the Christian community or an implicit faith that loves and serves him hidden in some other religion or way of life—will be born as well into this and be integral with this one new creation. What we talk about is the Body of Christ, a reality St. Paul frequently spoke of, a gift of God already realized partially but not yet in the fullness God intends.

The life of Jesus, the redeeming Christ, will be writ large in this Body. His story, which is the paschal mystery, is the foundational story of each of us. It is in this mystery that we are all called to make our Passover journey. Its pattern of dying and rising interprets the ultimate significance of the life of every one of us.

This mystery is also the same Divine Mystery of light and love that is emerging throughout history in the one, universal Body of Christ. Paul proclaims this ultimate point of history to be Christ, in which "God will be All in all." Teilhard affirms the same, calling this climax of history the omega point, the new creation in Christ, the divine milieu. He understands the divine milieu to be an environment or center in which we live and move and have our being. It is in this Mystery that we make our Passover journey, personally and as a people throughout all time.

In the introduction of this book I alluded to such a "transfiguration" as something that the apostles Peter, James, and John foresaw for themselves—and implicitly for all of us—when they were on Mount Tabor and saw Jesus transfigured. The picture of the crucified-risen Jesus radiating Divinity through his five wounds—already referred to in the discussion questions of the previous chapter—stands as a preview and glimpse of what will happen to us, personally and as the human race.

With the help of Teilhard, let us look more closely at the nature of this divine milieu or Body of Christ. It is first experienced as something vague, like an irrepressible source of all that is, of all life and energy. Yet, it is eventually experienced as personal with a life of its own, in which all mineral, plant, animal, and human life lives and moves and has its being. In those whose lives and desires give shape to faith in God's plan all opposites will have been reconciled; all traits in our lives and in human relations, while seeming contradictory or irresolvable, will be harmonized. All who tried to live in fidelity to the One who is Goodness, Beauty, and Truth, as best they knew this One, will be unified as a transcendent whole in Christ, while never losing their individuality.

When Paul says in Romans 8:22 that all creation is in anticipation of the coming glory of the sons and daughters of God, he is alluding to the God who is more and more emerging or shining out through us. He is pointing to the fullness of the human race's opening out into divine life with all of the purity and goodness of God, with the infinite capacity for living the life of God and doing the things only God can do. He is referring to "the perfect man," fully mature with the fullness of Christ himself, that the author of the Letter to the Ephesians (4:13) proclaims when envisioning the whole human race as the Body of Christ come to completion.

Some might ask about the relation of Jesus the earthly Nazarene to Jesus the risen Christ. Does Jesus get "lost" in this cosmic vision, or just where does he "fit" in it? It needs to be said that in passing from this life into the resurrection Jesus the Christ became cosmic. That is, he is still physically present to the human race but with new and radiant physical characteristics— still unmistakably a human being but transformed in the resurrection. As the Christian gospels show, he is no longer bound by our present limits of time and space but has opened out into the freedom of living and relating in the eternal, present moment and to every creature and all creation. His being the divine Word through whom everything was created constitutes the basis for his being the Christ and center of the universe. In passing into eternity he possesses a new relationship to matter. He is physically present but with a new kind of matter, transformed in the resurrection, filled with the transparency of the Spirit, and no longer subject to death and decay. By his resurrection he is the Reality and Source in which every other creature is saved and sustained. "Jesus is the Christ but Christ is more than the man Jesus because Christ is the Word . . . the One in whom every person . . . and all creation . . . bear an intimate relationship with God."[5] The title of Christ refers to the fullness of all that the historical Jesus was but points also to "the fullness of love incarnate . . . the Christ who is coming to be."[6] This transformation, then, in no way diminishes his or our own humanity. Forever will he be fully human and at the same time fully divine. And so too, because of him, we will be truly ourselves, fully human and at the same time divine. This mystery is true for him by nature, while for us it will be by a wondrous gift of God's transforming us after the pattern of his Son.

There is one great birthing process taking place in history, therefore. Thanks to the Spirit of Christ, the Spirit of Love guiding this unfolding, all of creation, human and otherwise, is emerging as the whole Christ. Because God in Christ identifies with us, one can say as well that God, in his kingdom, is emerging. In the end there will be one Christ, one Reality, God and all creation transformed in Christ, loving himself.

A Communion of Universal Personal Friendship

This divine birthing will make for a great communion of all those who, by the grace of Christ, are willing to be transformed and brought into this new creation. The Christian theology of the resurrection and communion of saints points to an infinite expansion of all the good and spiritually healthy, mature relationships and loves we experience in this life. It points to "a community of universal personal friendship." It also implies that "each person would actually know every other person in his or her unique personality and affectively affirm each one in herself or himself, even experience personal communion of love and sharing of lives with every one of them."[7] This would be not as they are now but as they would be capable of being once transformed in Christ.

Our longings for communion are the God-given energy that moves us and all creation to being freed from anything contrary to Christ, to becoming a new human reality. God is moving those who are willing to be transformed in Christ to become wholly mature: emotionally, intellectually, aesthetically, morally, religiously. Only these, once transformed, will be ready to be participants in this universal personal friendship and communion.

It is mind-boggling to ponder the expansion of "conscious awareness and power of attention" that would exist in this communion. Consider the greatness of heart and mind, "the un-imaginable psychic and physical strength and energy such [men and women] would have in order to live such lives without being overwhelmed and shattered by too much life and joy. Think of what an interesting and utterly good and lovable person each one would be. Think of all the interesting and beautiful things that would be going on in the mind and heart of each person and how open and understanding and appreciative each would be of everything in every other."[8]

What a "world" such a universal personal communion and friendship among persons maturely developed in Christ will make. No embarrassment, no fears, no self-centered concerns in sharing with others. No concerns about exhaustion over relating to each and all this way. No worries about the limitations of time and energy in this world of being able to relate this deeply to just a few people. In our heavenly state there will be none of these earthly limits. As John of the Cross insists, we will love as God loves and know each other in the way God knows. The Infinite, hinted at in our longings in this earthly life, will be the nature and manner of our relating to each other once we are transformed in Christ.

Yet to think of our life in the coming heavenly state in terms of specifically favorite activities we enjoy in this life (e.g., golfing, cooking, gardening) is, I believe, to fall prey to a certain literalism or fundamentalism. It would imply that heaven is just a better version of this earthly life except we do not have to suffer, we do not have to worry about getting fat, and, best of all, we do not have to pay taxes nor worry about growing old and dying.

There will be no time or space limitations, no physical limitations as is characteristic of human nature before we are divinized. This will be a new creation and a communal realization of the deepest thirsts of each human being, of all human beings, of all creation. Together, we will have become the Body of Christ in its fullness. We will relate to each other with an openness and generosity analogous to the way the Persons of the Trinity relate to each other: as beings in each other! It has been said of the Persons of God that "in a unique 'coinherence' or mutual inter-penetration, each of the Trinitarian persons is transparent to and permeated by the other two."[9] In the best of relationships in this life, we can have, perhaps, at best, vague intimations of such beauty and glory awaiting us.

As it is for the three Persons of the Trinity, so too each person's love with its uniqueness will make an irreplaceable contribution to this ultimate universal communion. Each communion of mutual love, whether of two people or more, will likewise make an irreplaceable contribution to this ultimate communion. Every person transformed in Christ will enjoy friendship, freed from all fear and self-centeredness, with every other person. And every friendship, freed from all fear and self-centeredness, will be open to and rejoice in the friendship of all other persons with each other. There will be a universal communion of friendship and love that never ceases in its fullness of being and love. We and the rest of creation will form one Christ, and God will be All in all. Yes, we will be billions of individuals, but not merely a sum or collection of all. Rather, each and all of us, bound by a new unity with the triune God, will ourselves be *a new unity with the same divine nature as that of the triune God.*

The Passover journey, therefore, concerns more than just individual transformation and divinization. It also points to the climax of all creation and how, with and through the resurrected Jesus, we will become "the cosmic Christ, the Living One at the heart of the universe."[10] "Heaven will be . . . a total entry into the caverns of Christ's heart, an infinite space for the Father"[11] and all creation. This journey climaxes, then, in the fullness of God's joy into which we, God's beloved children, are welcomed. Forever we will be one family, one people, forming in our collectivity "the unity of the reality of God and the reality of the world."[12]

A Simple Analogy

Perhaps we can gain a hint of this communion and the depth of joy and godly trinitarian love reflected in it through a humble example. Recall our sharing in a family reunion during a holiday gathering. Those who have raised families with all its joys and challenges, its "fun times" and agonies, can relate. To have one's children and grandchildren back home for a visit gathered around a meal of abundance can overpower our emotions. For some this kind of moment reminds them of the meaning and ultimate accomplishment of their life. It can fill them with tears of hope for the final reunion of their family with God, as well as the entire human race in God. It can occasion healing and reconciliation as well as renewal of love among family members. It is no wonder that one of the Bible's most striking images for heaven is that of the heavenly banquet.

What a communion will be ours as the spiritual energy of friendship and unconditional love flows among us all in the back and forth of receiving and giving, of being known and knowing, of being loved and loving. Might we say that the end result of this one great communion of endless mutuality can be likened to the explosion of a star in the cosmos? This communion never ends in its unfolding. It keeps expanding, just as today's astronomers tell us the universe keeps expanding outwardly, further and further with no known limits.

Another Simple Analogy

If a loved one who is now with God were to come back to us for just a few minutes and we would ask what it is like in the next life, he or she would most likely be speechless yet radiate a peace and joy and maybe stammer out the words, "I cannot wait for you to join us."

For such a person to describe what the next life is like would be more difficult than if we tried to explain to a fetus something of what he or she will experience in the world this little one is soon to enter. The child would have no comprehension in being told, "Someday you will drive a car and ride in an airplane; you will graduate from college, travel to some beautiful places, and enjoy a hobby. Someday you will celebrate your birthday with cake and ice cream and go to school and make many friends." The fetus would probably blink with no ability to imagine any of this, yet pick up on the excitement in our voice and know that this is a state he or she very much wants to enter.

In many respects we are, in relation to heaven, in a situation similar to the infant in the womb. Yet, if we are selfless enough and attuned to the world of friendship and relationship, we can then recognize important hints of the manner of the life God is promising us.

Mercy Has the Final Word

One of the more memorable attempts at conveying a sense of this great homecoming of all creation and the gathering of all those who have loved God throughout history is an Easter sermon delivered by St. John Chrysostom, a Greek bishop (d. 407). To frame his sermon St. John used the gospel parable of the vineyard owner's hiring people at different times of the day and at the end of the day paying each of them the same wage (Matt 20:1-16). John did this most likely to emphasize the generosity of God, extreme and objectionable to some, as well as the overwhelming joy of those who share in this feast. The sermon follows:

> Whoever you are, come, celebrate this shining happening, this festival of light.
> You, the devout, God's unshakable lover, and you the servant brimming with thanks.
> Come, walk into the joy of your Lord.

You who began before sunrise, come for your stipend. You who waited till nine in the morning:
the feast is for you.
And you, the not-till-noonday starter, do not hesitate; you shall not lose a thing.
You who began at only three in the afternoon, have no scruples, come!
And you who arrived just before sunset, forget you were late. Do not be bashful. Our Master is magnanimous and welcomes the very latest with the first.
He will not entertain you less, you of the eleventh hour, than you the dawn toiler. No, not at all.
To this one He gives, and on that one He showers rewards. Whether you were a success or whether you only tried, He will greet you, make much of your effort, extol your intention.
Let everybody, therefore, crowd into the exhilaration of our Savior. You the first and you the last: equally heaped with blessings.
You the rich and you the poor: celebrate together. You the careful and you the careless: enjoy this day of days. You that have kept the fast, and you that have broken it: be happy today!
The table is loaded. Feast on it like princes. The milkfed veal is fat. Let no one go hungry.
And drink, all of you: drink the cup. The vintage is faith. Feed sumptuously all: feed on His goodness, His sheer abundance. No one need think he is poor, for the universal empire is emblazoned, wide open for all.

No one need mourn uncountable falls, be they over and over. For forgiveness itself has reared from the tomb. No one need fear death; for our Savior Himself has died and set us free. He confronted death in His own person, and blasted it to nothing. He made it defunct by the very taste of His flesh. This is exactly what Isaiah foretold when he declared, "Hell is harrowed by encounter with Him."
Of course it is harrowed. For now hell is a joke, finished, done with. Harrowed because now taken prisoner.
It snatched at a body and—incredible—lit upon God.
It gulped down the earth, and gagged on heaven.
It seized what it saw, and was crushed by what it failed to see.

Poor death, where is your sting? Poor hell, where is your triumph?
Christ steps out of the tomb and you are reduced to nothing.
Christ rises and the angels are wild with delight.
Christ rises and life is set free.
Christ rises and the graves are emptied of dead.
Oh yes, for He broke from the tomb like a flower, a beautiful fruit:
the first fruit of those already gone.
All glory be His, all success and power . . . forever and ever![13]

Godly Goodness in the Great Communion

Truly, God is more generous than we could imagine, more loving
and generous than we might ever hope for. But so too those
transformed in Christ. How filled will our hearts be with the
traits of Christ's Heart, above all with his great and unexpected
mercy. Heaven will be marked especially with stories of forgiveness and reconciliation that echo the forgiveness Jesus extended
to the thief on the cross and to those who mocked him during
his execution.

One of the great principles of the Christian philosophy of love
is that love must share itself if it is to be faithful to itself. This
especially characterizes God and all who are transformed in
God. Thanks to the Spirit's empowerment of such unconditional
love and freedom when we come into our heavenly state, we
can rightly wonder at the ways in which we will imitate God
and do what God does. What might be ways in which we will
pour out ourselves? We can only wonder.

I wish to relate a moving example from recent times of a sign
of this new creation, what I am calling a "web of mercy." It hints
at something of the quality of life and relationships that will
characterize those who have come into this new creation, this
new transformed state of being.

In the 1980s a group of French Trappist monks established a
community at Tibhirine, a small village of Muslims in northern
Algeria. Nine in number, they chose to live their vocation in a

non-Christian setting as a sign of Christ while sharing in the lives of these simple people. Their intent was not to gain converts as much as to witness to the Gospel, to be Christ in the midst of people who reverenced the Qur'an as their sacred Scriptures.

In October of 1993 the Islamique Armé (GIA) sought to take control of the country and threatened to kill all foreigners who did not leave within a month. On December 14, only a few miles from the monastery, twelve Croat workers had their throats slit and died. The monks knew these victims rather well. On Christmas Eve members of the GIA entered the monastery unannounced. The prior of the community, Christian de Chergé, explained that he and the other monks were preparing for Christmas, were committed to peace, and were not interested in taking sides with them or the government. At the same time they were more than willing to provide urgent medical care to one of the wounded GIA soldiers.

In the days that followed the monks met for a number of community meetings to discern whether they would stay in Tibhirine or leave. Government leaders promised protection for the monks and church leaders were ready to give them a new location, but the monks declined both offers. They said that they saw both options going contrary to God's calling for them and their vows of stability. They reasserted their commitment to stay at Tibhirine and continue living their lives in love of their neighbors in Algeria. They thought that to leave would be to fail God and their very identity. Instead, they were choosing to be "vulnerable witnesses for peace and companions in solidarity with the local Muslim villagers."[14]

Soon afterward Christian composed a letter to his parents, siblings, fellow Trappists back in France, and even his would-be assassin. He spoke with extraordinary compassion and courage in the face of the distinct possibility of a violent death.

To his assassin Christian said "a-dieu" or "good-bye" till they would meet before God. He even wished him a blessing. He said he saw his approaching death as a moment to be in union with all those who had been and were dying violent deaths. By no means did he see himself as innocent of the spiritual ills around him; instead, he asked for forgiveness from God, from others, and even from his assassin. He would not own any sense of being a martyr since he feared this would too easily allow Westerners to have one more reason for blaming Islam, identifying it with fundamentalist ideologies of extremists, and avoid looking at their own involvement in violence.

Having lived in Algeria as a boy, since his father's military career had brought him there, Christian had witnessed Muslims at prayer and was moved by their reverence, their sense of the Holy, and their submission to God's will. His mother stressed that they were to be respected, since she said "they worship the same God."[15] His best friend was a Muslim, having defended him one evening in the face of a gang that threatened his safety. That friendship became such a spiritual treasure for him, especially when the next day the gang returned to kill his friend for having protected him, a Christian. He could not help but think of Jesus's words about there being no greater love than in giving one's life for another.

This was a decisive moment in Christian's life. He had to live the same way as his Muslim friend had done, in being willing and ready to lay down his life for anyone and for all. He had recognized in his friend the best of Islam as well as the Holy Spirit of Christ acting in and through his friend. He was moved to live the rest of his life in this Spirit, and he was doing so as a Trappist monk in a Muslim nation.

With death close to his door, he wrote his letter in the spirit of Jesus saying good-bye at the Last Supper (John 17). He said he hoped he would "see the children of Islam . . . as God sees them: radiant with glory. From Christian's perspective this [was] a radiance filled with the glory of Christ, [the fruit of his passion], and filled with God's Spirit . . . mak[ing] perceptible the kinship of religious others while delighting in the differences."[16] He went on to say a deep thank-you for the life he had been given and the blessing of being able to give it back with love to God and the people of Algeria.

The most remarkable part of his letter, however, was Christian's good-bye and thank-you to his murderer. Like Jesus forgiving his executioners while he was dying, he said this person was not truly aware of what he would be doing but was doing what he thought was the right thing. He called him his "friend of the final moment," the one who would allow him to imitate Jesus in laying down his life for others. In his letter Christian even imagined the two of them, in paradise together, as "happy, good thieves," if this should please God, the Father of them both. He saw neither himself nor the other as innocent but both as brothers caught up in the violence "that engulfs the other and brings about his death."[17] What mattered in the end was that both were blessed with forgiveness, thanks to Jesus's giving of himself on the cross.

Christian and six of the other eight monks were abducted on the night of March 26–27 of 1996 and killed on May 21. (The other two monks hid and avoided the kidnapping.) On June 4 the seven monks were buried on the grounds of the monastery. Grieving for them were many of their distressed Muslim neighbors who had grown to respect and even love them. What lives forever is the extraordinary Christlike act of these monks, especially that of Christian. His compassion and mercy especially show us something of our spiritual future, of the depth and purity of our relating to each other once we have been transformed in Christ and come home to this new communion, the new creation, to the one Christ loving himself.

We Become One Eucharist

Perhaps the most striking image Teilhard de Chardin highlights in *The Divine Milieu* when talking about the final union of all creation is that of the Eucharist. He envisions our communion being of the same order and as wondrous as the eucharistic transubstantiation of bread and wine into the Body and Blood of Christ.

Like bread in the hands of the priest leading the Eucharist, God places in our hands, one day at a time, our lives and that of others, along with the rest of creation. God calls us to have faith in him and in what he is doing in our lives and in our world. We are to keep in mind his promise of the "pleroma," to trust in the transformation of our lives and our world that the Spirit of the risen Christ is fashioning.

Like the priest at the Eucharist, we are to call down upon the elements of our daily life and the world the Spirit of God. God is committed to fill with divine presence whatever good and potential good is going on in our lives on any day. He is at work in these particularities, moving them toward and integrating them in this one Christ.

The prerequisite for this, however, is our faith in God's love and our trust in what he is doing in history. These virtues are what open the door of our heart and mind to recognize this ultimate miracle taking place in our midst. As our faith and trust in God mature, we recognize more and more this Mystery emerging in time and history, like yeast in bread dough.

The eye of our heart opens further and further to see what God sees. We are filled with joy and love and are moved to worship and adore as we contemplate ourselves and all creation being transformed. All of this we lift up to God and join with Christ's own offering of himself as we pray, "Through him, and with him, and in him, / O God, almighty Father, / in the unity of the Holy Spirit, / all glory and honor is yours, / for ever and ever"![18]

In the end there will be one host, one cup, one sacrifice offered by the church, the "whole Christ," to the Father. Like Jesus at the Last Supper, we as one Body will say, "It is with desire that we have desired to eat this Passover with you, to be with you in this heavenly banquet." The great day of the second coming of Christ will have arrived, a never-ending day. We and the rest of creation will have become Eucharist, a single host raised on high to the Father. We will be one Christ loving himself. All in this communion will relate to each other as Jesus did at the first Eucharist: "This is my Body, my whole self given for you and for all. This is my Blood, my life and whole being poured out for you and for all."

On the front cover of this book is a picture that captures something of this great mystery. It is a copy of a painting dated near 1380 from Osnabruck, Germany, and now kept at the Wallraf-Richartz Museum in Cologne. Containing the primary colors of red, green, and yellow, it is titled *Descent of the Holy Spirit*. In it we see the Spirit of God, represented by a bird carrying in its beak the eucharistic host of Christ, while at the same time hovering over the twelve apostles and Mary, the Mother of Jesus.

This image strongly suggests how all of humankind, in our becoming what we receive in the Eucharist, is converging toward Christ, the large white host in the center of the table, as the Source of everything. With the guidance of the Holy Spirit and the twelve apostles, especially through the sacred Scriptures, as well as with the prayers of the Mother of God, archetype of the church, we and all of creation are moving toward complete union in this Center, to the One who will be All in all.

All glory be to God now and forever. Amen!

Questions for Discussion and Faith-Sharing

1. Describe what has been, prior to your reading this chapter, your sense of what heaven will be like for all those in the communion of saints. Mention what has changed for you in your understanding, if anything, about life in the communion of saints, thanks to what you have read here.

2. What parts of the reflections in this chapter on universal personal friendship have you experienced in your own life?

3. What parts of the Easter sermon of St. John Chrysostom do you enjoy most? In what ways does the story about the monks and their decision to stay at Tibhirine touch you? And the letter their prior, Christian de Chergé, wrote—what does it inspire in you?

4. Might you pray the Mass differently because of the way the mystery of the Eucharist is explained in this chapter? In what ways?

5. What does the picture on the front cover say to you about God, about church, and about your desires and hopes for yourself, for the human race, and for the world?

NOTES

Introduction

1. This cap is a sign of humility in the presence of God and a reminder and symbol of one's being Jewish. In most cases it is men who wear it but some women do as well. It is circular in shape and about three to four inches wide.

2. Covenant in this biblical context refers to a binding relationship between God and the Hebrew people. It is a pact based on a commitment that carries with it promises and obligations and is intended to last forever. Both God and the people are understood to be bound by a solemn agreement to fulfill this commitment and specific obligations to each other.

3. A period of time spanning approximately 1300 BC to 1000 BC.

4. A period spanning approximately 800 BC to 50 BC.

5. Note well that the words "It is with desire . . ." are a literal translation of the original Greek text. The New American Bible translates this phrase by the underlined word: "I have *eagerly desired* to eat this Passover. . . ."

6. Karl Rahner (d. 1984), a Jesuit priest and German theologian, adopted this title or name for God while recognizing both how God is beyond all names and ultimately is mystery and how this Divine Mystery is the epitome of graciousness. Hence the name Gracious Mystery.

7. Michael Downey, *Altogether Gift: A Trinitarian Spirituality* (Maryknoll, NY: Orbis, 2000), 98–102.

8. The Spiritual Exercises are a set of meditations on the purpose of our life, on our sins and on God's mercy, as well as contemplations on

155

many of the gospel scenes describing Jesus's conception, birth, life, death, and resurrection. They are meant to be guided by an experienced director, not to be done on one's own.

Chapter One

1. "The King and the Maiden," in *Parables of Kierkegaard*, ed. Thomas C. Oden (Princeton, NJ: Princeton University Press, 1978), 40–45.

2. I am greatly indebted to John Shea for what he says regarding the Lord's Prayer in his wonderful lectures titled "The Our Father Prayer," available in CD form and marketed by ACTA Publications in Chicago, Illinois.

3. Carl Jung (d. 1961), a Swiss psychologist, is quoted to have said that so many people prefer to remain minimally conscious, i.e., not wanting to be very self-reflective nor engage their soul and its conscious and unconscious depths because of its challenges calling for conversion and growth.

4. St. Ignatius of Loyola (d. 1556) is a good example of this point. It was during his reading biographical sketches of the lives of St. Francis of Assisi and St. Dominic (and while he was recuperating for months from a serious leg wound sustained in military battle) that he began to imagine a new way of living his life. The inspiration of God through these two saints moved Ignatius to imagine for himself something of the same rich life with God that these saints modeled, something much more meaningful and consequential than the life he had been living.

Chapter Two

1. See Paul's Letter to the Romans, 7:14-25, for a description of his own experience of this fallen human condition. See also Thomas Keating, *The Mystery of Christ: The Liturgy as Spiritual Experience* (Amity, NY: Amity House, 1987), 35–42.

2. Paul Tillich, "You Are Accepted," chap. 19 in *The Shaking of the Foundations* (New York: Charles Scribner's Sons, 1948), 153–63.

3. See the Jerusalem Bible translation of Wisdom 2:24, where the fallen angels are said to have brought death into the world because they envied God.

4. See Paul's Letter to the Romans, chapter 3, in which he exclaims that because of Adam's sin, there is not one just person left, that each and all of us have fallen and need a redeemer.

5. See Psalms 41, 42, and 63 as they beautifully describe our soul's strong thirst for God.

6. Gerald May, *Addiction and Grace: Love and Spirituality in the Healing of Addictions* (New York: HarperCollins, 2007). See chapter 1 especially.

7. Peter G. van Breemen, "The Courage to Accept Acceptance," in *As Bread That Is Broken* (Denville, NJ: Dimension, 1974), 9–15.

8. "Lookin' for Love," a song made popular by singer Johnny Lee and featured in the 1980 movie *Urban Cowboy*.

9. See nos. 45–71 in David Fleming, SJ, *Draw Me into Your Friendship: A Literal Translation and a Contemporary Reading of the Spiritual Exercises* (St. Louis, MO: Institute of Jesuit Sources, 1996), 42–61. Ignatius of Loyola states in one of his many letters that in his opinion the source of our sinful ways is our ingratitude, our forgetting the blessings of the Lord.

10. Bernard of Clairvaux, *On Loving God* (Kalamazoo, MI: Cistercian Publications, 1995), 18.

11. Stanley W. Green, "When We are Reconciled, We are Free," *The Canadian Mennonite* 4, no. 17 (September 4, 2000): 11.

Chapter Three

1. Gregory the Great, Homily 2, *Forty Gospel Homilies*, trans. David Hurst, OSB (Kalamazoo, MI: Cistercian Publications, 1990), 11.

2. Andrew Greeley, *The Jesus Myth* (New York: Doubleday, 1973), 44.

3. Joachim Jeremias, *The Parables of Jesus* (New York: Charles Scribner's Sons, 1963), 145–46.

4. Monika K. Hellwig, *Jesus, the Compassion of God: New Perspectives on the Tradition of Christianity*, Theology and Life Series 9 (Collegeville, MN: Liturgical Press, 1983), 77.

5. See the Gospel of St. Luke, 10:42, where Jesus, while visiting his friends Mary and Martha, chides Martha for being so upset with her sister and says that Mary, sitting at his feet, has chosen the one thing necessary, single-hearted focus on Christ.

6. Hellwig, *Jesus, the Compassion of God*, 77–78.

7. Joachim Jeremias, *New Testament Theology* (New York: Charles Scribner's Sons, 1971), 219–30.

8. David Fleming, SJ, *Draw Me into Your Friendship: A Literal Translation and a Contemporary Reading of the Spiritual Exercises* (St. Louis, MO: Institute of Jesuit Sources, 1996), 84.

9. Ibid.

10. Ibid., 86.

11. Ibid.

12. Ibid., 82.

13. Marianne Williamson, *A Return to Love: Reflections on the Principles of A Course in Miracles* (New York: HarperCollins, 1992), chap. 7, sec. 3, pp. 190–91.

14. Fleming, *Draw Me into Your Friendship*, 82.

Chapter Four

1. This word appears numerous times in all three of the Synoptic Gospels to refer to the source of Jesus's power in his ministry. Examples are Matthew 7:29; Mark 1:27; and Luke 4:36. When *exousia* is taken apart, separating the word into *ex* (meaning "from" or "out of") and *ousia* (meaning "Being" or "the Source of all that is"), we get the meaning of "from Being" or "from the Source of all that is," namely, "from God." It is in this sense that the people meant Jesus to be one who spoke with authority, or from God and God's depths.

2. *Dunamis* also appears numerous times in describing the results of Jesus's ministry; see two instances in Luke 4:14, 36.

3. See no. 109 in David Fleming, SJ, *Draw Me into Your Friendship: A Literal Translation and a Contemporary Reading of the Spiritual Exercises* (St. Louis, MO: Institute of Jesuit Sources, 1996), 94ff.

4. There is significant flexibility in the ways people make the Exercises of Ignatius. Some make them over thirty days while withdrawing from their usual daily routine and living at a retreat center or in some other quiet setting. Each day the retreatant meets with his or her guide/ director to share the fruit of his or her prayer in the last twenty-four hours and then receives guidance for the coming twenty-four hours. Much more often, people, while still engaged in their usual daily life and work, devote a period of prayer each day to some part of the Exercises for a number of months, usually eight to ten. They will see their guide usually once a week. The time for prayer each day can vary from as little as one-half hour to a full hour. The retreatant and his or her guide can come to a mutual decision on this matter. Having a guide is essential to a good and valid experience of the Exercises.

5. Fleming, *Draw Me into Your Friendship*, no. 109, pp. 94–95.

6. Ibid., nos. 124, 125, p. 100.

7. Ibid., nos. 111–26, pp. 96–101.

8. I recall one female retreatant being so moved with maternal love that she saw fit to nurse the Christ infant.

9. To learn more about this kind of prayer read the simply worded, short paperback titled *The Contemplative Way*, by Franz Jalics, SJ (Mahwah, NJ: Paulist Press, 2011). Also, the excellent writings of Frs. John Main, OSB, and Laurence Freeman, OSB, available through the World Community for Christian Meditation. So too the writings of Fr. Thomas Keating, OCSO, available through Contemplative Outreach.

10. Sermons (de Scriptura) 88, v. 5, quoted in John Main, OSB, *Word Into Silence* (New York: Paulist Press, 1981), 28.

11. Fleming, *Draw Me into Your Friendship*, no. 124, p. 100.

12. St. John of the Cross, *The Spiritual Canticle*, stanza 12, in *The Collected Works of St. John of the Cross*, trans. Kieran Kavanaugh and Otilio Rodriguez (Washington, DC: Institute of Carmelite Studies, 1979), 453–57.

Chapter Five

1. David Fleming, SJ, *Draw Me into Your Friendship: A Literal Translation and a Contemporary Reading of the Spiritual Exercises* (St. Louis, MO: Institute of Jesuit Sources, 1996), no. 97, p. 86.

2. Ibid., 113.

3. Ibid., 113, 112.

4. Ibid., 112.

5. I am grateful for a number of excellent reflection questions posed in relation to St. Ignatius's Two Standards Meditation by Jacqueline Syrup Bergan and Sr. Marie Schwan in their *Birth: A Guide for Prayer* (Winona, MN: St. Mary's Press, 1985), 56–69. This volume is the third of five in the Take and Receive series.

6. Ibid., 63, 64, 68.

7. Nos. 149–57 in Fleming, *Draw Me into Your Friendship*, pp. 116–20.

8. Cf. "paracletos" in *A Lexicon, Abridged from Liddell and Scott's Greek-English Lexicon* (London: Clarendon Press, 1953), 523. To liken the Paraclete to a defense lawyer suggests that Satan is the prosecutor, accusing us and citing all our sins in front of God, as he did to Job. The Paraclete defends us before the throne of God, pointing to Jesus's redemptive act at Calvary, and prays for us, "Lord, have mercy!" while declaring us to be washed and redeemed in the blood of the Savior.

9. Thomas Keating, *Fruits and Gifts of the Spirit* (New York: Lantern Books, 2000), 15, 23.

10. Ibid., 15.

11. Ibid., chaps. 4–6.

12. Francis Kelly Nemeck and Marie Theresa Coombs, *The Way of Spiritual Direction* (Collegeville, MN: Liturgical Press, 1985), 95.

13. Ibid., 99.

14. A sacrament is a holy sign or symbol through which we perceive and receive an invisible grace or blessing from God. Christ is the primordial instance of this encounter with God. In him God's saving mercy becomes effective in human beings needing salvation.

15. Icon is a Greek word meaning a sacred image or picture representation of God or a holy person.

16. Such interior, intimate knowledge comes through encountering Christ, mediated through the interior senses of our soul, as was described in chapter 4. This knowledge, a gift of the Spirit praying in us, comes when we spend significant time contemplating the pierced side of Christ and entering his Heart. Saint Thomas the Apostle found there all he needed to live courageously for Christ and eventually to lay down his life for him. It is there that the Dominican mystic Catherine of Siena (d. 1380) says we will hear God share the secret of Jesus's Heart: "I have allowed his side to be pierced in order to reveal the secret of his Heart, which I have made a hidden refuge where you are permitted to see and to taste the ineffable love which I have for you" (quoted in Edouard Glotin, SJ, *Sign of Salvation: The Sacred Heart of Jesus* [New Hyde Park, NY: Apostleship of Prayer, 1989], 22).

17. St. Augustine (d. 430) and numerous other Fathers of the church recognized this connection, understanding the pierced side of Christ in a mystically rich sense as well as in its historical facticity.

18. Jerome Murphy-O'Connor, *Becoming Human Together: The Pastoral Anthropology of St. Paul* (Wilmington, DE: Michael Glazier, 1982), 56.

19. Donald Senior, *Jesus: A Gospel Portrait* (New York: Paulist Press, 1992), 22.

20. Frank Andersen, *Making the Eucharist Matter* (Notre Dame, IN: Ave Maria Press, 1998), 21, 22, 29.

21. Andersen emphasizes the act of drinking the Blood of Christ. In doing so we speak in a public way our yes to the covenant with God to be a people distinguished by justice and compassion. We drink into ourselves the Word of God we just heard. Ibid., 26–29.

22. Spoken by Pope Benedict XVI at a General Audience in Rome, August 12, 2009.

23. *Lumen Gentium* 53, in Austin Flannery, ed., *Vatican Council II: Constitutions, Decrees, Declarations; The Basic Sixteen Documents* (Collegeville, MN: Liturgical Press, 2014).

Chapter Six

1. Teresa of Ávila, *The Interior Castle*, in *The Collected Works of St. Teresa of Avila*, vol. 2, trans. Kieran Kavanaugh and Otilio Rodriguez (Washington, DC: Institute of Carmelite Studies, 1980), 341–45.

2. See James A. Krisher, *Spiritual Surrender: Yielding Yourself to a Loving God* (Mystic, CT: Twenty-Third Publications, 1997), for an excellent, practical exposition on this theme.

3. Teresa of Ávila, *The Interior Castle*, VII, 4, p. 446.

4. All four gospels record this: Matt 26:69-75; Mark 14:66-72; Luke 22:54-62; John 18:15-18, 25-27.

5. St. John of the Cross, *The Dark Night*, in *The Collected Works of St. John of the Cross*, trans. Kieran Kavanaugh and Otilio Rodriguez (Washington, DC: Institute of Carmelite Studies, 1979), bk. I, chap. 10, sec. 6; also bk. II, chap. 5, sec. 1.

6. See John of the Cross, *The Ascent of Mount Carmel*, in *The Collected Works*, bk. I, chap. 4, sec. 2; also chap. 6, sec. 1.

7. This is what St. Ignatius of Loyola proposes for the retreatant making the Spiritual Exercises. The retreatant is to confront his or her sin and do this while face to face with Jesus on the cross.

8. See *Ascent of Mount Carmel*, bk. I, chap. 2, for three reasons why John calls the spiritual journey a dark night.

9. John of the Cross, *Dark Night*, bk. I, chap. 8, sec. 3.

10. John of the Cross, *Ascent of Mount Carmel*, bk. II, chap. 8, sec. 6.

11. John of the Cross, *Dark Night*, bk. I, chap. 14, sec. 1–4.

12. Francis Kelly Nemeck and Marie Theresa Coombs, *The Spiritual Journey: Critical Thresholds and Stages of Adult Spiritual Genesis* (Wilmington, DE: Michael Glazier, 1987), 108–13.

13. John of the Cross, *Dark Night*, bk. II, chaps. 5–10, esp. chap. 6, sec. 1.

14. Walter Ciszek, *He Leadeth Me* (Garden City, NY: Doubleday, 1973). See especially chap. 7.

15. John of the Cross, *Dark Night*, bk. II, chaps. 5–8.

16. Ibid., bk. II, chap. 10, sec. 6.

Chapter Seven

1. Jürgen Moltmann, *The Crucified God* (London: SCM, 1974), 276.

2. David Fleming, SJ, *Draw Me into Your Friendship: A Literal Translation and a Contemporary Reading of the Spiritual Exercises* (St. Louis, MO: Institute of Jesuit Sources, 1996), nos. 165–68, esp. nos. 167, 168: "The Three Kinds of Humility," pp. 128, 130. Also Brian E. Daley, SJ, "To Be More Like Christ: The Background and Implications of Three Kinds of Humility," *Studies in the Spirituality of Jesuits* 27, no. 1 (January 1995).

3. Joseph A. Tetlow, "A Readjustment of Life," in *Choosing Christ in the World: Directing the Spiritual Exercises of St. Ignatius of Loyola According to Annotations Eighteen and Nineteen* (St. Louis, MO: Institute of Jesuit Sources, 1999), 164.

Chapter Eight

1. St. John of the Cross, *The Dark Night*, in *The Collected Works of St. John of the Cross*, trans. Kieran Kavanaugh and Otilio Rodriguez (Washington, DC: Institute of Carmelite Studies, 1979), bk. II, chap. 10, sec. 1. Note: Three outstanding commentaries on the works of St. John are *John of the Cross for Today: The Ascent* by Susan Muto (Ave Maria Press, Notre Dame, IN); *John of the Cross for Today: The Dark Night* by Susan Muto (Epiphany Association, Pittsburgh); *The Impact of God: Soundings from St John of the Cross* by Iain Matthew (Hodder & Stoughton, London).

2. John of the Cross, *Dark Night*, bk. II, chap. 10, sec. 2.

3. Ibid., sec. 4.

4. John of the Cross, *The Living Flame of Love*, in *The Collected Works of St. John of the Cross*, st. I, sec. 22. Further citations of this work are given in the text.

5. John of the Cross, *Dark Night*, bk. II, chap. 10, sec. 7.

6. John gives here a lengthy explanation of why people do not progress to these deeper, more mature stages of prayer and life with God.

7. John acknowledges that he is mixing images here when describing aspects of the same reality. He says that "this fire . . . is so gentle that, being an immense fire, it is like the waters of life, which satisfy the thirst of the spirit with that impetus the spirit desires. Hence these lamps of fire are living waters of the spirit . . ."

Chapter Nine

1. St. Augustine, Homily 10 on the First Epistle of John 3, in *The Works of St. Augustine* III/14, trans. Boniface Ramsey (Hyde Park, NY: New City Press, 2008), 148.

2. Pierre Teilhard de Chardin, *The Divine Milieu* (New York: HarperCollins, 2001), xiii–xiv.

3. Regis Martin, *The Last Things: Death, Judgment, Heaven, Hell* (San Francisco: Ignatius Press, 1998), 163, quoting Hans Urs von Balthasar, *Credo: Meditations on the Apostles Creed* (New York: Crossroads, 1990).

4. Pedro Arrupe, "Centre of the Christian Mystery," *In Him Alone Is Our Hope: Texts on the Heart of Christ* (St. Louis, MO: Institute of Jesuit Sources, 1983), 90. Arrupe is quoting Teilhard de Chardin from his journal, cahier VI, p. 106.

5. Ilia Delio, *The Humility of God: A Franciscan Perspective* (Cincinnati: St. Anthony Messenger Press, 2005), 107.

6. Delio, *The Emergent Christ: Exploring the Meaning of Catholic in an Evolutionary Universe* (Maryknoll, NY: Orbis Press, 2011), 50.

7. Jules Toner, *Personal Friendship: The Experience and the Ideal*, an unpublished manuscript, chap. 11, pp. 2–3.

8. Ibid., chap. 11, p. 4.

9. Gerald O'Collins, *The Tripersonal God: Understanding and Interpreting the Trinity* (New York: Paulist Press, 1999), 132. See also Iain Matthew, *The Impact of God: Soundings from St. John of the Cross* (London: Hodder & Stoughton, 1995), 120: "Father, Son and Spirit are each absolutely poor because they each give themselves completely—so utterly rich with the other's generosity . . . [and all of creation is] the fruit of an excess of [this] unselfishness."

10. Delio, *The Humility of God*, 107.

11. Matthew, *The Impact of God*, 127.

12. Delio, *The Humility of God*, 164.

13. Paul Roche, trans., "Easter Sermon of St. John Chrysostom," *America* 143, no. 13 (1980): 282.

14. Karl A. Plank, "When an A-Dieu Takes on a Face: The Last Testament of Christian de Chergé, OCSO," *Spiritual Life* 53, no. 3 (2007): 146.

15. Ibid., 143.

16. Ibid., 144.

17. Ibid., 146.

18. Doxology prayer, which concludes the Eucharistic Prayer in the Roman Rite of the Mass.